PARENTING HAPPY TEENS
IT'S AN INSIDE JOB

Dr. RJ Jackson
Teen Life Coach

RHG | MEDIA PRODUCTIONS™

What People Are Saying

"Helping teens and their parents focus on living and creating a life with purpose and meaningful goals, this book is must-read for adults, teens, and everyone in between!"
    —Wendy K. Benson, MBA, OTR/L and Elizabeth A. Myers, RN
    2x2 Health: Private Health Concierge

"As a retired teacher, I believe this book should be recommended reading for all parents and teens. It is an easy-to-read book that is chock full of practical wisdom for everyone. The skills taught in *Parenting Happy Teens* help to develop self-confident, successful, and happy adults."
    —Elda Robinson, Retired Teacher

"Working in higher education for 21 years, I have seen a shift in what teens think when it comes to achieving success and happiness. Dr. RJ targets where the heart is when it comes to building confidence and accurate thinking within teens. If you have a tween or teen at home, the time is now to read *Parenting Happy Teens: It's an Inside Job.*"
    —Sonja Montiel, M.A., Founder of College Confidence and Co-Founder of The DH Effect

Contents

Welcome

Dear Parent/Mentor of Teens,

I present this book to you because I want any teenager, anywhere in the world, to have the opportunity to feel happy and successful—inside and out!

You support the teen you love with encouragement to improve their grades, activities that position them well for college or a career, rewards for doing their chores, paying for tutors and coaches, and offering them other incentives to accomplish the stuff we all believe they need to accomplish—all good!

YET...we adults are missing a key piece to this puzzle of adolescence that will make all the difference in teens' *true* success (and, by the way, our peace of mind).

What is the missing piece?

Our teens' thoughts.

Do parents really want to lecture, cajole, reward, bribe, argue, and punish to ensure their teenagers become productive, happy adults?

I don't believe they do.

This book is about getting BEHIND the reasons why teens are not maximizing their potential, why they make choices that don't serve them, and why they are experiencing so much stress, worry, and unhappiness. What I'm about to share with you will help your teen shift from struggle into self-responsibility, motivation, confidence—and more self-love—all of which becomes the foundation for accomplishment, success, and happiness.

When teens understand the patterns of their thoughts, feelings, and emotions, they realize how they are driven by those patterns. They learn they actually have control over their thoughts and can manage them, which puts them right smack in the driver's seat to achieve their most meaningful goals.

This means they are motivated to accomplish things for themselves, with LESS prodding and pressure from parents and other adults. They develop confidence and trust in their own capabilities. They experience mastery, resilience when things don't go their way, and reason to celebrate their successes—because they know how AWESOME they are.

It's personal growth for teens, and it's powerful stuff!

In my decades of working with teenagers, I can tell you straight up teens are READY for this inner work. They really do want to get along with their parents, they want straight A's, they want to excel, they know how to work hard, and they don't want to be pushed or punished or pressured.

Teenagers WANT to have meaning and purpose in their lives. The teen years are critical because this is when foundations for adulthood are built. What better time than adolescence to teach and nurture the important values that will guide our teens through the rest of their lives?

That's why I've written this book and why I'm so glad you're here!

Warmly,

Dr. RJ Jackson

Introduction

You are right to be concerned about your teen

Let's face it, life today can be tough for a teenager. American teens have a lot on their minds, according to researchers including a recent Pew Research Center survey of youth ages 13 to 17.[1] Seven in ten teens say anxiety and depression are major problems among their peers. Serious depression in teens has been on the rise in recent years.[2] The bombardment of electronic media has magnified social challenges for teens such as: bullying, drug and alcohol use, body image issues, academic problems especially in the post-pandemic transition, peer pressure (in person or online, like sexting), on-screen violence, and unsettling uncertainties about global concerns like social inequities, climate change, and world health.

On a daily basis, middle and high school students must try to manage their time among schoolwork, sports, friendships, hobbies, projects, family time, and so on. As much as it's difficult for parents to admit, today's teens also deal with issues at home due to divorce, poor communication, mixed messages, difficult moves, a parent's job loss, witnessing or being on the receiving end of abuse, and more.

It's a lot for teenagers to handle!

All these real and perceived problems can become obstacles that stand in the way of a teen's success and happiness.

With all teens have to deal with, they can often feel burned out, leaving some with a sense of unfulfillment. This results in a lack of motivation, with little interest in learning, contentious relationships, stress, anxiety, and more. Couple these factors with all the external expectations and temptations from society, and it's no wonder teens are faced with real issues and challenges!

---

[1] https://www.pewresearch.org/social-trends/2019/02/20/most-u-s-teens-see-anxiety-and-depression-as-a-major-problem-among-their-peers/
[2] https://www.samhsa.gov/data/sites/default/files/NSDUH-FFR1-2016/NSDUH-FFR1-2016.pdf

The bright (and exciting) side

But let's change the picture and see what else adolescence has to offer: new adventures every day as teens discover aspects of themselves that move them from "kids" to "adults." Academic studies open their minds to information and insights that introduce them to broader levels of life outside their own little worlds.

They begin to excel, accomplish, and compete in ways that are exhilarating and devastating (exciting either way!). They are exposed to life lessons that guide them through adulthood and impact their success and happiness. They develop friendships and deeper relations with their families that they'll cherish all their lives.

And, c'mon, they are standing on the threshold of an amazing life journey, preparing to jump and soar!

This book is for parents about teenagers. The information I share does not ignore the real statistical challenges adolescents face today. Rather, my purpose is to address what is often NOT taught in school or at home. It's what is INSIDE them that teenagers need to learn—and what parents need to know to support and guide them through that learning.

I offer concepts and practices (and games!) that will give your teen the foundational preparation to create their future with confidence, self-love, meaningful goals, better communications leading to better relationships, control over their academic success, and leadership of their own destiny.

These lessons will embed ***resilience, positivity, purpose, and happiness*** in the young person transitioning to adulthood. They are my core principles in my life coaching work with teens.

This is my message to parents, guardians, educators, mentors, and supporters of teens: ***success and happiness are an inside job.***

Why me?

From the smiles guy to the teen whisperer

It all started around 6th grade when I discovered I had a heart to help others. I was the person whom other kids felt comfortable talking to and sharing things. I look back now at how devastated I would feel after hearing student after student tell me how unhappy they were.

At my middle school I created the first-ever *Student Talks* program, where for 15 minutes a day, students were given the opportunity to speak to teachers, coaches, and guidance counselors about life. With the success of the program, I committed to a lifelong mission of spreading happiness.

When I sat with my high school guidance counselor to talk about what degree I wanted to pursue in college, I had no idea. I just told her I liked to make people happy, and I wanted to make the world smile.

My counselor gave me two options:

1. Become a comedian
2. Become an orthodontist

As you probably have figured out, I chose option number 2. I founded my orthodontics practice, and I was in the business of creating smiles—great!

Although the school counselor gave me great advice, she never mentioned a third option to make the world smile, which was ***becoming a life coach***. I could help people smile from the inside out.

A few years into my orthodontics practice, I was asked by a patient's parents if I would coach their teen on some issues he was facing. As a result, this teen became a more confident person and a straight-A student. I began mentoring youth in my free time while more and more parents were requesting my coaching for their kids.

Apparently, I was the Teen Whisperer! The intuitive talent I discovered back in sixth grade still made teens feel safe and comfortable with me, sharing things they couldn't tell anyone else (including their parents). They knew I had their back, and we worked together through thorny problems, explored questions, and celebrated great improvements.

I was so gratified by these successes, that I got hooked. I became a certified Teen Life Coach—one of the few in America—and I have coached many different types of challenges teenagers face at home, in school, in their activities and relationships, and preparing for their future after high school. I coach both individually and in group calls (where I have over a hundred teens on the line from all over the country), teaching life skills behind the immediate issues kids face during adolescence—so they can shift their thinking and beliefs, become a leader in their own decisions and lives, and become happier.

We can put a band-aid on a problem a teen is facing (which is important to do for sure), but my core principles go beyond that: *I give them the insight and skills that help them flourish in today's world and throughout their lives.*

Now, not only do I create smiles on the outside, but I also focus on creating smiles on the inside.

What is a teen life coach?

I tell my parents and teenagers that a life coach is like your football, lacrosse, or baseball coach. They teach the skills to help you succeed, and that's what a teen life coach does.

While a lacrosse coach will teach you skills necessary to win games, a life coach will teach skills necessary to win in the game of life.

A piano teacher will teach you skills to excel in music. A life coach will teach skills that help you excel in all areas of life—to trust your capabilities, to handle success and bounce back from failures, to have exciting, meaningful goals that give you purpose and accomplishment, to understand what success truly means and that it is yours to have.

Parents will ask me: what is the difference between life coaching and therapy?

Often parents seek out therapy if they notice anything wrong with their child. In many cases therapy has its place. Some teenagers need therapy. Some need medications.

However, life coaching has completely changed the way we view mental health in teenagers. There is not always something "wrong" with the child or something that must be diagnosed. For the majority of issues teens face, life coaching can be the preferred option. My coaching program is personal, positive, and goal-oriented. I create a safe space for the teen to share their struggles and questions with me—they know I have their back, but of course I'm working with the parent too, so we are a team working together.

I have seen where my life coaching has brought a teen out of a depressive period, averting a potentially more dangerous situation for them. Dealing head-on—and early on—with struggles can make a BIG transformation in a teenager's outlook and vision of the future.

It's huge for a teen to know there is a trusted adult like me on their side, with the expertise and care to guide and teach them along the way.

Why would a teenager need a life coach?

Life coaching can help with:

Time Management. I believe if you were to poll 100 parents and ask them to rate their teens' time management skills, 99% would say "needs improvement." That's when you know it's time to teach time management! There is a reason that college students struggle with the same problem. A teen life coach can help your teen develop a plan to succeed in all areas, thus increasing their ability to succeed post-high school and developing a sense of fulfillment.

Self-Esteem/Confidence. It's quite normal for students to value their friends' opinions more than their parents'. You may think the world of your child but if their peers think differently, then your teen might see themselves as having less value, as "not enough." A life coach is not only a positive voice to remind your teen of their unique and special abilities, but the coach also identifies and challenges the negative self-talk that allowed a teen to think less of themselves in the first place.

Goal Setting/Problem Solving. Teens generally know what they like—well, sort of! I have found most teens are not clear on what they want. A life coach will help your teen create a plan to achieve each goal they desire. We teach them problem-solving, resilience, and motivation skills that help them focus on goals and overcome obstacles that stand in the way of their success.

Navigating Life in Adolescence. Even the best parents are often the LAST people teens want to go to—part of a teen's job is showing independence on the path to becoming an adult. The teen life coach is trained to step in as that crucial, outside, adult influence. Sometimes teens need to hear the same thing you've been preaching to them from someone else! Perhaps they just need to hear it in a different way—who knows? The point is it won't hurt to plant more than one seed of wisdom and guidance into an ever-developing mind.

What do we ultimately want for our children?

One word: **Happiness**. Wouldn't you agree? Now, here's the thing: We can't "create" happiness or "make" our children happy. Happiness is a *state of mind*, something each of us must figure out on our own—and many aspects of happiness can be learned.

I think about a study that shows on average, a baby smiles four hundred times a day while adults smile fewer than 20 times.[3] As a teen life coach, I'm interested in what happens between babyhood and adulthood that influences the desire to smile out of happiness.

Especially since the 1990s, bodies of research by psychologists and neuroscientists have shown that some people have a *happiness state of mind* carrying them through life, no matter their circumstances. From studying happiness, I believe the following are the top-of-the-list qualities all happy people share:

Confidence—happy people believe in themselves, their goals, wisdom, worth and power.

Positive thinking—happy people make conscious decisions to counter negative thoughts with positive ones like hope, wisdom, love, inner power, and joy.

Engagement—happy people take part in activities that bring them joy and positive energy.

Relationships—happy people build close social ties and loving relationships with friends and family.

Meaning—happy people have a sense of purpose and a sense of something bigger than themselves.

Accomplishment—happy people create and achieve positive goals they believe in.

---

[3] https://www.thejournal.ie/mental-health-smile-1550017-Jul2014/

Gratitude and giving to others—happy people appreciate the gift of life, and generously volunteer to help others.

All my work, including this book, is founded on helping teenagers learn the happiness mindset—true happiness where they love themselves, have confidence, express their full potential and innate talents, create a life with purpose and meaningful goals, enjoy beautiful relationships, face any challenge with resilience and hope, and flourish in a life full of joy and gratitude.

Smiling on the inside as well as the outside! #SmileInOut

How to use this book

Parenting Happy Teens: It's an Inside Job is divided into four sections. You can read through from start to finish, or choose a section that's particularly important to you.

Section I: Confidence 101. Topics include: why confidence is so essential; how our thoughts work to bring us results; how negative thoughts keep us from thriving and how to shift them; limiting beliefs and how we can identify, overcome them, and create new beliefs that speak joy, love, happiness, forgiveness, and all that lifts us up. Tips for you to support your teen in these areas.

Section II: Understanding and Living with Emotions. Topics include: The difference between feelings and emotions; how we can use the messages our feelings and emotions are giving us; choosing clear and healthy perceptions; ways to process and handle disappointments and to stay resilient; and a deep look at anxiety, anger, and depression in teens. Tips for you to support your teen in these areas.

Section III: Relationships and Communication. Topics include: what are teens thinking; what teens wish their parents would do; truths about parent-teen relationships; how to improve your relationship with the teen; helping teens understand different perspectives; communication skills for teens and for parents. Tips for you to support your teen in these areas.

Section IV: Goals, Success, and Happiness. Topics include: why teens need to have meaningful goals; learning the power of "intrinsic motivation;" what exactly IS success and how to define it for themselves; ways that teens are leaders and influencers in everything they do; what happiness is and how to cultivate a happiness state of mind; how happiness factors into pursuing one's goals; happiness allows us to be who we were created to be. Tips for you to support your teen in these areas.

In these chapters you'll find the best of the lessons I teach my teens. These life lessons and skills for personal development are based in adolescent psychology, framed with my own spin to make the teachings relevant to teen lives, on a level they can understand.

As I said, there will be games—you'll see we have a little crazy fun sometimes. I hope you will find this information helpful, not only to support your teen but also to use in your own life. After all, the learning doesn't stop when we leave high school, right?

Teen Talk

Interspersed throughout the chapters are real-life examples of my coaching conversations with teens, called "Teen Talk." These excerpts will help illustrate the concepts I'm sharing, and give you a "fly-on-the-wall" look at what teens like yours say, feel, and explore. I'm sure you'll find THAT enlightening!

The Teen Talk content is taken from individual teen and parent coaching, and from my live, online teen group life coaching seminars, *Life Coaching with Dr. RJ*,[4] which I broadcast weekly.

Please note: To protect the confidentiality of my teens, Teen Talk segments excerpts have been modified or are composites of different conversations with common themes. All teens' names have been changed.

A word about "A Teen's Perspective"

A Teen's Perspective is a live coaching seminar for teens, the first of its kind. Teens from all over the country come together to help each other succeed.

---

[4] https://ateensperspectivepodcast.com/

I'm the creator and moderator. I not only facilitate discussions and share tips and strategies, but I also coach students "live" in leadership and personal development.

Personal development is extremely important at this age, even though it is not part of most education curricula or therapy. That's why I say "happiness is an inside job." Adults who focus on personal development learn that happiness starts on the inside. They realize the pursuit of *things* to "make" them happy or relying on *people* to bring them happiness are not recipes of a happy, fulfilled life.

These life-affirming realizations come late in some people's lives, and for many, not at all.

What if teens could learn from adult mistakes and start personal development NOW? Imagine if they did not have to follow the typical path of most humans, chasing one mirage after another for years and years!

No surprise—teenagers typically do not show an interest in "personal development." I find the main reason is simply a lack of awareness. It's just not discussed, and it's rarely encouraged. Many students, like many adults, believe personal growth happens naturally over time.

Unfortunately, we only have to look at the condition of our world to see that personal development is not a natural process. It takes focus and lots of practice. If teens can start the process now and make a habit of focusing on personal development, life will be more fulfilling, and they will experience more success.

Are you ready to change everything up for your teen and for the world?

I KNOW your teen is ready to become the person they want the world to see, so let's make some smiles, inside and out!

If you believe you and/or your adolescent could benefit from life coaching, use this code to schedule a consultation.

SECTION I

Confidence 101

CHAPTER 1

Confidence is All in Your Head

As a certified life coach for teens, I have coached every issue that teenagers face. Believe me, I've heard every story! And here is what I have concluded: Most of the issues teenagers face stem from a LACK OF CONFIDENCE.

Even straight-A students or athletic superstars can lack confidence. They may feel confident around their friends but not in larger groups. They may be confident in math but have fears about mastering physics. They may be confident at practice but "choke" when the game is on the line. They may feel confident generally but never "enough" to meet their parents' expectations.

According to authors of a 2018 study out of Trakia University, Bulgaria, "High self-esteem has no positive effect on school performance. A study even showed that artificially inflated self-esteem leads to poorer school performance."[5]

Why wouldn't a teen who is high-performing, active, and "successful" not be confident? In a study of over 5,400 teens, why did 95% report feeling inferior at some point in their lives?[6] I believe this gap is because confidence needs to be developed. Teens especially need support in developing and growing their confidence regardless of how "successful" or "not successful" they—or we—think they are.

Confidence is something that is developed and practiced

Confidence is not something "lucky teens are born with" or someone naturally acquires with maturity. If your child is NOT actively developing their confidence then your child is NOT confident. At least not on the level of

---

[5] source: https://www.researchgate.net/publication/326944270_Self-esteem_in_adolescents
[6] https://www.stageoflife.com/StageHighSchool/OtherResources/Statistics_on_High_School_Students_and_Teenagers.aspx

the deep self-awareness and self-love that will support them throughout their lives, no matter what they face.

If confidence is something that needs to be learned and practiced, then when does a teen take that "class"? In most households, I bet the topic doesn't come up at the dinner table or is taught like driving a car, folding laundry, or good study habits, right? Understandable! This is because it's an "inner game" kind of thing that typically isn't taught in school or at home (except by example, which of course is very important).

Confidence begins in the mind—which can be changed

A teen develops confidence through thoughts and beliefs. If she believes girls are bad at science, it's likely she won't get good grades in science classes, or even take them at all. If he loves basketball but believes he's too short to play, he won't practice or try out for the basketball team, or even go out for any sports at all. In the study I cited above, the top three reasons teens reported feeling inferior were: appearance (59%), ability in some activity (49%), and intelligence (38%).[7] Doesn't that sound to you like perception rather than fact?

Here is an excerpt from my live coaching sessions with teens:

Teen Talk

Dr. RJ: Did you know that life happens in your mind? I'm not talking about a sci fi movie! Your experience of life is based on how you think. If you change the way you think, you could change your experience of life. Whether we think life is amazing, fun, boring or *I don't like life at the moment*—it's all based on what we're thinking about. The same thing can happen to two people, yet they see it in two different ways, they

---

[7] https://www.stageoflife.com/StageHighSchool/OtherResources/Statistics_on_High_School_Students_and_Teenagers.aspx

take different actions in response, and they get two different results.

Here's an example of how powerful your thoughts can be—AND a huge confidence boost! Let's say you are dreading studying for your history test because you believe you're not good at history, remembering all the dates and things. Your grades have been pretty good, but you're not confident you're doing well enough.

Why do you have to stick with that thought? Who decided you aren't good at history? YOU did! So being good at something is your opinion, isn't it? What if you changed your mind? Why not start believing you're GREAT at history, maybe even LOVING it. Let your thoughts begin to say that you are good at it. Start smiling when you're doing your history homework and studying for the test. Tell your friends and family that history is your favorite subject.

What do you think might happen?

[Teens respond in online chat space]

Yes, great answers! You get an A on your test, and you realize you actually like history and you are confident in your ability to rock it!

This is the power of your thoughts. And, believe me, I see it happen all the time in teens just like you.

When I asked the question, *did you know life happens in your mind*, not one of the kids on the call had thought about life in that way. They are in the process of learning about the power they have over their lives, that **their view or interpretation of life isn't the only option** (knowledge adults might take for granted). So when they experience a poor grade, a friend who doesn't invite them to their party, bullying, their parents getting divorced, any blow to their self-confidence (you get the idea), they believe THIS IS IT. THIS is my life.

Think about what happens when kids realize they have the power—superpower—to affect their own response to life! The awareness alone is a confidence booster. I go on to give them an illustration of this concept and exercises to use it. It's something you can also use to help your teen to learn and practice confidence. I call it the "Thought Triangle."

The Thought Triangle

My "Confidence 101" teaching is based on the idea that a teen's experience of life begins with their thoughts and beliefs. To illustrate this concept, I created the **Thought Triangle**.

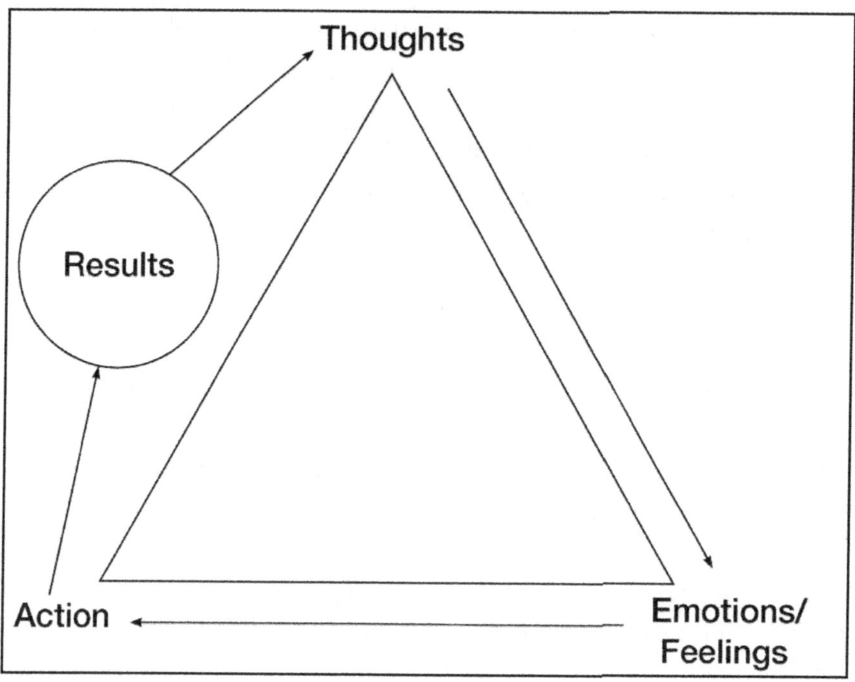

Here is how the Thought Triangle works. At the top are "THOUGHTS"—they run everything. "Thoughts" influence "EMOTIONS/FEELINGS" (the second point on the triangle), and this in turn creates ACTION (the third point of the triangle). The ACTION causes a RESULT which in turn affects THOUGHTS. And the cycle continues, for better or for worse, depending on the nature of those thoughts.

A group of thoughts make a BELIEF. The belief system influences actions, which causes results. Thoughts influence feelings, which influence your actions, which ultimately give you a result (something you want—or something you don't want).

When teens see this connection, they understand the power of their thoughts and that their world isn't just one reality, but has many options and perspectives. I present it as "triangle offense" (I'm a basketball player!) because teens need to know they don't have to be passive, submissive, or on defense. Once they realize they have thoughts and beliefs that bring down their self-image and mess up their results, they can take action (be on the mindful, proactive offense) to change results to ones they want.

How do we use this tool? Here is real-life example from an online coaching session with a teen I'll call "Raymond":

Teen Talk

Dr. RJ: Okay, everybody, to see how the Thought Triangle works, I asked you to give me an example of a time when you were extremely mad. Raymond tells us he's mad at his mom because he thinks she's controlling the schedule he worked out for the pandemic and online school. She's asking him to do stuff when she wants it done. When he follows his schedule and still gets everything done, she calls him lazy. She never listens to him anymore so there's no point in even trying.

So we go to our Thought Triangle with Raymond's thought: My mom doesn't listen to me anymore. The feeling makes Raymond mad and frustrated too. And maybe he feels his mom doesn't care about him.

Raymond, let's look at the "action" point of the Triangle. What was your action whenever you were upset? What did you do?

Raymond: Before the pandemic I could take myself out of the situation, hang out with friends, go skating and stuff. But now, getting away is a lot harder to do.

Dr. RJ: I hear you. So you get mad, but kind of avoid the situation.

You talked before about the relationship with your mom. It sounds to me like you want a great relationship with your mom. We could call this the "result." Listen to how the Triangle works:

If you have thoughts that say, my mom doesn't care about what I have to say, she doesn't want to listen to me, then it's going to make you feel mad and frustrated. In terms of action, there are a few things you can do—choose to avoid the situation by doing nothing.

Everyone, if Raymond does nothing about the relationship, what is the result going to be? Will it be the great relationship that he wants?

[Teens respond in online chat space]

No—I agree. So this is a natural process. It's how life happens in your mind. Your thoughts control your feelings, and your feelings control your actions, which are going to give you the result that, in a way, you "created." An unwanted result leads to thoughts again...and guess what? They're the same thoughts that got you into this negative situation!

We went on to investigate the statement Raymond made about his mom not listening to what he has to say. I suggested there was no way to confirm the statement because we're not in his mother's mind. It's just the way Raymond believed she made him feel (which is a natural response). We don't know if it's true—it's an guess. If he had a different guess, a different interpretation of his mother's actions, what might that be like?

What if the thought was that Raymond's mom works so hard to take care of the family, she sometimes gets burnt out? *She's really working hard, and she cares about me, and she really wants to know what I have to say. She's just super tired.*

We explored what Raymond's new feelings might be because of the NEW thought. Maybe he'd feel kind of bad for his mom, or feel grateful that she does so much for him. We tried these on for a few moments.

Raymond's next action might be to help his mother out, making her life easier in some way. The result would be them having a better relationship. I tell the group that it takes two people to be in relationship, but one person can influence that relationship. Another action Raymond could take is to ask his mom for what he wants, maybe a promised block of time when he can do whatever he wants without interruption, something they can work out together.

It's a beautiful thing to witness the shift in these kids when they're invited to see things a little differently, to dig a little deeper into what might be really going on with their situation, and feel more power over their thoughts, feelings, actions, and results.

This is just one example of how the Thought Triangle works, how it shifts our thoughts, actions, and the way we perceive and react to others. It's a tool you can use to help your teen think through a situation they are struggling with.

Advantages of being confident and why it's so important

Hey, who am I to say these teens even *want* to be confident?

We adults can make some off-track assumptions about today's teenagers—what they want and what's important to them—because we see them through the lens of what the world was like when we were their age. They live in a different world and I try to remember to listen carefully and avoid assuming anything!

So I asked teens on a group coaching call if they thought there were advantages to being confident. It was great to hear that, yes, they did, and many shared the advantages they saw in being confident: *Happier. More friends. People will approach you. People respect you. To help other people to be better. Self-image, better self-esteem.* Beautiful, isn't it?

Self-confidence is one of the most important teachings I have for teenagers. Why? Because I want them to realize their greatest potential, and the key to that is CONFIDENCE. If they don't believe in themselves and their ability to go after what they want in life, then they will never have the motivation, focus, resilience, or vision to make their dreams come true.

A person who doesn't have confidence on the INSIDE doesn't show up confidently on the OUTSIDE. Their thoughts (self-doubts, not enough-ness, hopelessness, self-criticism, self-judgment) lead to emotions and actions—or inaction—that do not move them forward to achieving their potential. They don't outwardly display the qualities that would inspire others to help and support them. It becomes a self-sabotaging cycle that continues to hold them back from achievement, self-expression, and happiness.

Remember, no matter a teen's background or successes, if they don't feel self-confident INSIDE, then they won't act confidently. With our help, they can learn how to develop confidence skills and a mindset that will help them tap into their potential.

In this same group coaching call, I told the teens what I believe is the biggest advantage of confidence: *reaching their full potential.* When they're confident, they will tap into their full potential—full-bodied and all in—to fulfill the purpose they were created for!

Teen Talk

Dr. RJ: You are one of a kind, and there's something special you're supposed to do. Confidence will help you do it. If you second-guess yourself or lead a life based on other people's expectations, you won't take the path that is uniquely yours.

Close your eyes right now and imagine you are confident—whatever confidence means to you. Imagine you're not worried about what anyone else thinks of you and what you should do and who you should be. You are unique and unstoppable. Imagine a great idea pops into your head and you just try it—whatever it is! You invent something new, start a YouTube channel, draw something amazing. Just sit and imagine it for a moment—soak in the act of creating something, anything big or small, and you have every reason and resource to make it happen.

How does it feel? That's what believing in yourself looks like. You can accomplish amazing things, but you must be confident.

It's important for teens to not only intellectually understand why confidence is important but feel it too. The more senses they use to understand and recognize confidence, the more proactive they'll be in building it.

FEEL it and ACT it to BE it

We adults can admit we don't feel confident ALL the time. Walking into a boardroom to present your first project as a new hire. Holding your newborn baby in your arms and wondering what kind of parent you will be. Stepping onto the field to compete in a game or exercise or physical challenge you love. All these situations can lower your confidence level fast, at least for a few moments.

Because teens face so many new life experiences and milestones, all while their bodies and brains are developing into maturity, the expectations of adulthood are smack in front of them all the time. And let's not forget their emotional ups and downs and the unpredictable mood swings. So there is a lot of potential for confidence-sapping situations.

What do adults do to pump ourselves up with confidence when we need it?

How we THINK is a powerful resource, as shown by the Thought Triangle. The exercise I did with the teens to IMAGINE being confident is a winner because it helps teens physically ACT and FEEL confident in their body and bones.

Another exercise I do with my teens is called the Mirror Affirmation, which can be fun for some teens and difficult for others. I ask them to stand in front of a mirror and look at themselves (I tell them it might feel embarrassing at first and that's okay). I have them talk out loud to their reflection saying positive statements such as: *I am smart. I am a leader. I am loved.* Anything they think will boost their confidence.

For homework, they are to do this twice a day for a period of days, or as long as it takes for them to feel a change—I'm happy if they do it every day until they don't feel they have to anymore. The Mirror Affirmation helps teens overcome self-doubt. It literally rewires their brain to have new beliefs that lift them up in positive ways. They already learned the concept of the Thought Triangle and the power of thoughts and beliefs, so they know it can work. Things start to change for them—small and big successes—and every time they notice, share, and celebrate them, their beliefs strengthen even more.

Final thoughts on confidence: Teens will tell me they're not confident because they're shy, or "bad" at something, or it's just their personality. They use these words in a definitive, limited way—they believe they ARE this thing.

This is not true! They are not "stuck" being a definition they created or, worse, that someone created for them. I tell my teens that ***"confidence" is an*** *emotion based on beliefs—that's all. It's how they feel, not who they are.* Thoughts, beliefs, and belief systems can be changed.

This is a BIG distinction to understand (which you'll see in Section II on emotions), and I hope the adults around our teens understand it too. Otherwise, our teenagers are going to grow up "boxed in" by definitions that have been given to them, quashing their own beliefs, dreams, success, and happiness.

How to develop and support your teen's self-confidence so they feel proficient and adept:

1. Help them practice awareness of feeling confident. Because confidence is an emotion everyone can have, let your teen know they can *practice* feeling and being confident at any point in time. Support them in identifying what confidence feels like and encourage them to KEEP practicing so they can GET USED TO being confident.

2. Model confidence for your teen. Your kids are learning confidence from you, so model confidence even if you're not quite feeling it. Being highly prepared and optimistic when tackling new tasks sets a good example for your teen.

3. Support awareness of choosing what they believe about themselves. Your teen may believe they aren't confident, or that they're shy or incapable. The belief might be something they embraced in elementary school. Remind them (kindly and without judgment) they are a completely different person now. What they *were* is irrelevant and what they can *be* has endless possibilities!

4. Don't make every mistake a big deal. When your teen makes a mistake, don't be upset. Encourage them to see we all make mistakes, and the important thing is to learn from them. A confident person is not afraid of "failure," but knows how to take it in stride.

5. Show them confidence isn't bragging or thinking you're superior to others. It's an inner emotion of self-awareness, self-esteem, and self-love. When we feel these things on the INSIDE, we can't help but show them on the OUTSIDE, and the effect is contagious in the best possible way.

CHAPTER 2

Inner Thoughts That Tear Us Down

As our teens' world expands and they begin to have more experiences and gather more knowledge, they learn their actions have consequences. They're exposed to other ways of thinking or perspectives different from their own. Teens become aware of their own thoughts which can be confusing or even scary. Add hormones into the picture, and no wonder teenagers can feel anxious, stressed, lacking in confidence, overwhelmed and even depressed.

Because they're in the thick of it, teens often aren't even aware of what's going on inside of them, or why it's happening! My role as a coach is to call out and address confused thoughts and feelings, so we can look at them in the light and understand them together. The mix of things going on in teens' minds begins to make sense, or at least teens realize they are not alone or weird, or that their whole lives will be like THIS.

Your teen should not be alone with their thoughts

My message to parents: *Your teen should not be alone with their thoughts.* They need help managing their thoughts in a complex, sometimes dangerous world where so many negative influences pressure them at such a young age. I'm sure you have seen the spiraling black hole a teen can go down—just from a slight at school, a poor grade, something tragic in the news, or an argument in the family. When they're in that hyper-emotional hole, they have trouble stepping outside of those thoughts. This is what leads to bad decisions like self-harm, binge-drinking, and more.

"Emotion regulation skills develop substantially across adolescence, a period characterized by emotional challenges and developing regulatory neural circuitry," say the authors of a study on positive and negative emotion regulation in adolescents.[8] One of their findings suggests that *emotion regulation skills* may help a teen work through adversity in their early life. The better their emotion regulation skills the better they will manage or avoid troubles in their adult life.

The pre-teen and teenage years are a crucial time of development, when kids learn to process their thoughts, feelings, and emotions on a neurological level—literally! As the adults in their lives, we have an incredible opportunity to help them develop these skills.

The "positive" and "negative" thoughts that develop our beliefs

"Teens who can describe their negative emotions...are better protected against depression than their peers who can't," finds a study on negative emotion differentiation (NED), published in the journal *Emotion*.[9] Therefore, understanding emotions and regulating them are important skills we can teach and support in our teens. Let's help teens better understand, describe, and regulate their thoughts, feelings, and emotions.

In my view, there is much more research about so-called "negative" emotions than there is on "positive" emotions. We need to find a way to balance this out, and help our teens choose a more positive and confident outlook in life.

This is the basis of my work with teens: I believe adolescence is the time for a person to form an outlook on the world that will lead them to happiness.

Each kid has so much potential. They are smart, funny, and hardworking. They have dreams and ideas and creative genius to share. My vision is to help them focus on everything that makes them feel good, has them feeling excited and motivated about goals they've created, and equips them to reach their full potential.

Teens usually come to me when they feel troubled, and we work together to resolve issues they are struggling with. However, my coaching doesn't stop after the "crisis" is resolved. I'm mainly about exploring the positive with them:

---

[8] https://www.ncbi.nlm.nih.gov/pmc/articles/PMC6523365/
[9] https://www.sciencedaily.com/releases/2019/06/190628120447.htm

- What can they love about themselves?
- How can they choose thoughts that lift them up, not tear them down?
- How can they shift negative beliefs about themselves into positive ones?

When our teen is caught up in their emotional black hole of anxiety, confusion, fear, sadness, or low confidence, they're left feeling bad about themselves. Enter the Thought Triangle: Emotions trigger thoughts, which form beliefs, all of which have them believing "not enough-ness" and the vicious cycle perpetuates.

I work with my teens to uncover the effect their thoughts have on their beliefs—identifying them, naming them, unpacking them, and making an informed choice of accepting or rejecting them. We start with their "Inner Villains."

What are Inner Villains?

I tell teens that negative thoughts such as hate, selfishness, revenge, anger, and envy can drag us down. These thoughts give them the urge to fight with a friend, argue with their parents, cheat on a test, bully the new kid, or spread rumors about a classmate. ***These thoughts prevent their mind from growing and keep them from being who they were created to be.***

Positive thoughts can help us thrive. They speak joy, love, happiness, forgiveness, and other good things. When these thoughts affect our behavior, our mind grows. Positive thoughts make us feel good about ourselves and good about our life.

Negative thoughts do the opposite. "Inner Villains" are the voices in our heads that tell us *we are not enough.*

- *I'm not smart enough.*
- *I'm not pretty enough.*
- *I'm not strong enough.*
- *I'm not creative enough.*
- *I'm good, but not good enough.*

It's not only teens who hear those voices during their lives, is it? Our Inner Villains may not say those exact things to us, but it's still the core of the message *I am not enough*. We adults may procrastinate doing our work because we believe we're not good enough to succeed at it, or strong enough to cope with failure. We may skip exercise because we feel we'll never be fit, thin, attractive, enough. We may push our kids into achievements that we (subconsciously) believe we weren't good enough to succeed at ourselves.

I realized who my main Inner Villain was during a time when I was having a lot of success (Inner Villains can be tricky like that). Life was great and I was about to start my own orthodontist practice, ready to launch it with a huge celebration. Well, it took me eight months to open the practice and during that whole time, I never created the big celebration!

Why would that be? Because my self-talk was: *Now I've got to get to work. I've got to get to this next goal.* Then it was the next goal, and then the next, and I kept going like that. Evidently, I believed I didn't deserve celebration until... what? I suddenly realized THIS was my Inner Villain—yes, I was successful, but the voice in my head kept telling me I couldn't celebrate because I hadn't accomplished enough. I wasn't enough.

By the time I realized what was happening, it was too late to create the celebration I'd been thinking about. But I realized I had to stop going and going and going to reach an elusive, impossible definition of "enough." As I often tell my teens, **all experiences are opportunities for growth**.

Now that I have children of my own, I'm practicing more and more how to say goodbye to that Villain, to pause, stop, be present, and enjoy the beautiful moments of my life—which are MORE than enough!

I shared this story with my teen coaching group, and went deeper into the Inner Villain concept with them:

Teen Talk

Dr. RJ: Today we're going to talk about Villains. This might be a hard one, so be prepared! Everyone has what I call an Inner Villain, just like mine in my story. It's the voice in your head that tells you you're not enough. Why would you have a voice that does that?

Well, the Villain believes it's keeping you safe. It lives in the part of the brain that's designed to protect us, to keep us from touching a hot burner on the stove, to tell us to run when we're in danger. It's like a biological switch in our brain whose job is to keep us alive.

That's an important function, isn't it? But, in the process of protecting us, the Villain's voice can limit us. It can hold us back. It might think it's keeping us from doing something because it doesn't want you to be embarrassed or hurt. Why? Because your beliefs tell you if you take a risk, or stand up in front of people, or whatever the action is, you'll embarrass yourself or someone will say something hurtful to you.

We've talked about how our beliefs and thoughts aren't always facts and not always helpful to us, remember?

So the Inner Villains in our head can make us believe things that aren't good for us. Here's one way to understand how it works: Remember when you learned how to ride a bike. Imagine that your parents never let you take off the training wheels—ever! They say they're trying to protect you: We don't want you to fall and hurt yourself. They mean to help but they're not.

You don't want to use training wheels on your bike all your life, do you? You want to depend on your balance and ability to steer that bike on your own, even if you fall off sometimes. That's one way to view the Villain—he's not a bad guy, really, but the things he tells you don't give you the freedom to be and do what you want.

Why is all of this important? Because your thoughts determine how much success you'll achieve, how much happiness you'll have when you reach your full potential!

Your Inner Villains are the reason you don't have the things you want—good grades, excellence in sports, making good friends, having a loving relationship with your parents, getting into the college or the job you really want. Take the training wheels off. The point is YOU ARE ENOUGH, so let's find those Villains!

How do Inner Villains show up?

When teens begin to understand how their subconscious thoughts can sabotage them, they realize how thoughts become beliefs that reinforce feelings of "not enough-ness." Next we want our teens to identify the nature of these Inner Villains so they can see them for what they really are—thoughts or beliefs that may not be true and don't support them.

I see three main types of Inner Villains that show up most often:

Inner Villain #1: Any thoughts, whether random or associated with some event, that trigger saying or doing something negative to others. If a teen's belief is they are not enough, not significant, not lovable, they subconsciously deflect any risk of others reinforcing that belief by proactively behaving negatively toward others or sabotaging themselves. Examples:

No one really wants to get to know me because I'm not [smart, popular, fun, interesting] enough. This belief makes a teen say negative things to potential friends, pushing them away and avoiding the risk of being hurt or embarrassed in the future.

My parents don't [listen, respect, love] me. This belief makes a teen try to get more attention, but it's often negative attention. They do and say angry things for no apparent reason. They believe they're not good enough to excel or be accepted, so they quit rather than risk failing or being embarrassed.

I enjoy doing [theater, dance, tennis, etc.] but they're all so toxic so I quit. A belief that quitting or not trying at all is a better choice than risking exposing themselves to failing, or not measuring up to their own expectations.

Inner Villain #2: Negative thoughts that focus on a person or, more often, on themselves. A teen's negative thoughts can repeat in their heads so much, they begin to believe the thoughts are true. Teens are not aware they have been convinced, because they haven't fully developed discernment yet, so they believe without questioning.

Examples:

I have never made straight A's in my life, so I can't now. If they never did it before they won't be able to do it now. This belief has an "all or nothing" aspect, meaning they could make almost all A's but don't believe that.

I'm not smart enough so I won't do well on the test anyway. This belief leads to procrastination in doing homework or studying, blaming the teacher, or comparing themselves unfavorably to others, all of which sabotage their confidence in themselves.

I love [gymnastics, basketball, tennis, etc.]! But everyone keeps telling me that I'm [too small, too tall, too thin, too heavy] to succeed at it. This belief thrives from listening to others, or making assumptions without questioning what's true or possible.

This Villain can cause teens to obsess about something. For example, getting addicted to video games to keep up with their friends, or extreme dieting to lose weight fast and fit into a prom dress.

Inner Villain #3: Negative thoughts about the future because of assumptions about the past. Something bad happens to the teen that is completely out of their control, either far back in their past or recently. The Villain keeps the teen in that moment, feeling their future will always have those same consequences or results. The teen feels out of control and the fear can become overwhelming. The assumption about the past then becomes a belief about the future.

Examples:

My parents got a divorce, and I feel like it's my fault. Nothing's certain anymore. I don't feel safe and I just can't count on anything. This belief keeps teens stuck in guilt, sadness, and feelings of uncertainty about their future.

The pandemic has me feeling so scared about sickness and death. The future will always resemble the past. Feelings and thoughts a teen has now cannot be changed to more hopeful ones about their future.

I had an injury as a young kid caused by [swimming, horseback riding, soccer, etc.] I loved to do, and I'm not going to try it again even though I'd loved it so much. A belief develops that because of a past negative experience associated with a positive activity, talent, or achievement; any future attempts will have the same outcome.

This Villain is a tough one because it causes teenagers a lot of anxiety, stress, worry, and sometimes depression. I advise teens to ***notice when they feel negativity or fear of the future,*** and I offer some behavioral warning signs:

- They don't look forward to tomorrow, feeling dread when they wake up in the morning.

- They feel a lack of motivation about things they used to enjoy or goals they want to achieve.
- They get addicted to something—their phone, playing video games, snacking, etc.

Here is an effective response to all these thoughts: NO ONE knows the future. The truth is *they are creating their future all the time* so they get to choose what it's going to be and how they will respond to anything, "good" or "bad," that happens to them. This is powerful information!

The secret to finding thoughts that hold you back: pay attention!

Identifying Inner Villains empowers teens to understand why they sometimes say or do things they don't feel so good about later.

The next step is to support teens in learning to separate the thoughts they want to keep from the thoughts that drag them down and tell them *they are not enough.*

Here's an overview of the process I take my teens through. The point is to develop the skill of **PAYING ATTENTION.** This seems simple, but it's actually something both teens and adults can forget. It requires concentrated action and takes commitment and consistent practice. After all, thoughts which have repeated in our heads for months and years are not easily expelled from our minds.

I talk to my teens about the difference between thoughts and beliefs, and facts. For example: It is a fact that your parents got a divorce. But the thought that it was your fault, or now you're not loved as much, or your life is not certain nor safe anymore—these are NOT FACTS, but *opinions your Inner Villain has been telling you.*

Here is the process I walk my teens through (by the way, it's the process I used to conquer my own Inner Villain!):

1. Pause and notice when you are feeling happy or unhappy. Try to discover the thoughts that cause you to feel this way. Do this multiple times during the day until you become used to it. (Tell your teen it's a practice the same as practicing piano or football or anything else you want to get good at).

2. Twice a day, write down those thoughts. Spend about 10 minutes writing about thoughts you noticed, once after work/school and again before you go to bed. By doing this, you will be able to capture your thoughts from the two most influential places in your life. (Your teen can treat it as taking notes for a class.)

3. Pick one thought to work on. Choose a thought that consistently shows up. Write it down in a sentence that starts: "I am not enough because [I'm too tall, not smart, my parents don't love me, work/school is too hard, I can't make friends, I never succeed]..." Now write an opposing, positive sentence: "I am enough because I'm tall and can play center on the basketball team." "I am enough because my parents show their love for me by [making dinner every night, working hard to make money for the family]..." "I am enough because I'm smart and can do well in all my classes."

4. Practice changing negative thoughts into positive ones. You may not believe your sentence at first. But practice saying your positive sentence to yourself and notice how you feel (the Mirror Affirmation exercise works well here). Just small steps toward believing it are powerful. The more you truly believe the opposite of a negative thought, the more powerful your thoughts will become, and the more you will take actions that make an impact in your own special way!

I encourage practicing together with your teen so you can support each other in using powerful and positive language that leads to positive actions.

How to help your teen work with negative thoughts

1. They can wire their brains for a positive outlook. This is a crucial period in your teen's development when they are learning "emotion regulation skills," so much of this information and experience is new to them. Your message: *You have the superpower to understand and manage your thoughts. You can wire your brain to make better decisions and have a positive outlook on your day, your week, and your life.*

2. They are enough. Help your teen notice how they feel after they say or do something that tears someone down, or how they feel when they notice negative thoughts about themselves. Your message: *The negative thoughts repeating in your head make you believe you are not good enough, even though you are! When you do or say something and you don't feel good about it afterward, it means you listened to negative thoughts instead of listening to your true self, who ALWAYS supports you in positive ways.*

3. They are making choices. Help them choose wisely. Have them share with you the successes they experience when they make positive choices. Your message: *When you practice paying attention to your thoughts, you become aware of how they influence your actions throughout the day. Thoughts can change the way you treat your family, your friends, your classmates, even strangers—in a positive or negative way. You get to choose how you respond!*

4. They are amazing. You know your teen is amazing! They know you know it too, and that you love them. Still, they can easily go down the emotional black hole, as you've probably seen them do. Your message: *You are really good at telling the difference between facts, and thoughts and beliefs. You can tell when your Inner Villains are hanging around, and you know they're there to limit you, not protect you. Thoughts that make you feel unhappy will cause you to forget you are unique and special. The more time you spend on thoughts and actions that make you happy, the more you'll impact your world in a positive way—in your own special way!*

5. Journal their thoughts. Do the "pay attention" exercise together—maybe journal together and take turns turning a negative sentence into a positive one. Your message: *Writing down your negative thoughts and turning them into positive sentences is really helpful and can ease your mind. You might want to get a special notebook or journal just for this practice.*

CHAPTER 3

Limiting Beliefs Limiting Potential

What is a limiting belief? I explain it to my teens this way: A belief is an opinion that can't be proven but you really think it is true, and any belief that keeps you from unlocking your potential is a limiting belief. The key is this:

- Uncover the beliefs we have so that we can see which ones are limiting us, and then reject them.
- Look for the beliefs that make us feel good and support us in achieving great things for ourselves.

"Beliefs turn into self-fulfilling prophecies," says therapist Amy Morin, writing for *Inc.com*.[10] "Unhealthy beliefs lead to unhealthy habits. And unhealthy habits produce negative outcomes that ultimately reinforce your unhealthy beliefs. It's a vicious cycle that can be tough to break." These cycles can start in childhood and go on throughout our adult lives, creating so much unnecessary struggle and unhappiness.

Everyone, not just teens, has a limiting belief or two, and will continue to have them throughout their lives. I sometimes tell teens my own story as an example: how I became an orthodontist because I wanted to impact the lives of teenagers. I figured if I gave teenagers a perfectly straight smile, then they'd have amazing confidence. I believed this would be my job forever.

As I began to get to know my patients, I learned more about what was behind their smiles. They often shared what was going on with them—the worries they had, the issues they were facing, situations they didn't know how to handle. Soon, parent after parent was asking me to work with their teen on an issue. I knew what most of them needed was a life coach, but I rarely could find one to recommend.

I don't have to tell you the direction this story takes—eventually I asked,

---

[10] https://www.inc.com/amy-morin/3-types-of-unhealthy-beliefs-that-will-drain-your-mental-strength-make-you-less-effective.html

why not me? And the answer was…my limiting beliefs: *I am an orthodontist. I can only discuss teeth. What are my colleagues going to say?* After wrestling with it for a while (even as my wife encouraged me to go for it), I could see it was just a belief that wasn't true and it was blocking me from my purpose and potential.

The rest, as they say, is history, and I couldn't be happier!

"Why does this have to be true?"

Some of us have limiting beliefs and know it right away. Other people's limiting beliefs are hidden in their subconscious, and they aren't aware how these thoughts are impacting their daily lives. For teens, limiting beliefs may hold them back from getting high grades in school, from participating in sports, from growing a deeper relationship with a best friend—or even making friends.

"Josie" believed she was unable to do well in online school. It was new technology to figure out, a routine at home to create, lots of unknowns, all without the support of her friends by her side. She felt like everyone else knew what to do and she wasn't going to figure it all out. She would make a fool of herself on screen and fail everything.

Here is how our teen group call helped Josie work through her limiting belief:

Teen Talk

Dr. RJ: Josie, let's talk about your limiting belief about succeeding in online school. Here we go—you're ready for it! If any of you have limiting beliefs in online school, what do they look like?

[Teens respond in online chat space]

Dr. RJ: Great answers, everybody—you don't know how you're going to do. You're nervous about it. You think you're not good at it. You're afraid you'll miss assignments or mess up the online class schedule.

So let's ask ourselves what this online school situation. But let's first think about asking a CONSTRUCTIVE question. We want answers that will help us not hurt us, don't we?

For example, if you ask yourself, why do I look ugly today, your mind is going to answer, well, look at your hair. Look at what you're wearing. Look at that pimple on your face.

What happened? You asked a question FROM your limiting belief about your appearance, so the answers you got back confirmed the belief. Not helpful, right? And not true!

So Josie, here's a better question to ask yourself about online school: What advantage do I have now in online school that I never had before?

Josie: I have more time to do more activities. I'm more focused. It's more convenient. I get to stay in bed longer in the morning.

Dr. RJ: Perfect, because the fact is that teens need more sleep during adolescence, and the teen brain wakes up later than when you were a child.

Now we know some things about online school we can do to succeed—practicing better focus, taking a break to do fun things, feeling more refreshed from a good sleep, and many more I know you'll think of. Does that help you feel more excited about school?

Josie: Very excited.

Dr. RJ: Perfect!

It's satisfying to watch these teenagers be willing to try new ways of thinking about their situations and lives. It's so much easier for them to start these practices now, while they are developing their identities and independence—before damaging beliefs become vicious cycles in their adult lives.

What an amazing chance we have to help teens address their limiting beliefs and unhealthy thinking habits, and give them a head start for a more successful, happier adult life!

How to overcome limiting beliefs

While I offer the following steps to help you work with your teen, I also hope they will help with your own limiting beliefs. I'm here to say it is definitely working for me!

Step 1: Identify the belief. Go back to the Thought Triangle: Beliefs cause emotions, which cause actions, which create either good or not-so-good results. This gives a foundation, a context, to explore what the belief might be—because there's going to be either an emotion or a result attached to it.

Example: *You truly believe you aren't good at making friends. So what happens when you get the opportunity to meet a new person? If someone approaches you, you feel super nervous, afraid you'll say something weird. So you just walk away, you withdraw. How do you feel afterward? What result are you getting from responding that way?*

Step 2: Question the belief. I challenge the limiting belief by having teens ask themselves two key questions: *Why does this have to be true? What evidence do you have that it's true?*

Example: *How many people have you gone out and tried to be friends with? How many friends do you believe someone has to have? Is it true we only have the capacity for [x] number of friends? What if your nervousness has nothing to do with the ability to make friends? Maybe you didn't have anything in common with the person, or the timing was wrong, or you have an image of what friendship is supposed to look like (from social media, TV, or movies) and maybe this isn't the way things really are.*

Step 3: Shift the belief. When we challenge limiting beliefs, we see the facts and realize there are more than a few ways to look at the results. Now teens are invited to choose the opposite belief: *I'm amazing at making friends!* (Like the work we did with our Inner Villains in Chapter 2, flipping our "I am not enough" statements to positive ones).

At first it often feels like a "fake it 'til you make" exercise, but as teens practice, they see the truth of limiting beliefs more clearly. They notice they show up a little differently, perhaps their head held higher, instead of turning away when someone approaches. They begin to feel comfortable looking people in the eye. They start looking for potential connections in activities they like, where they're more likely to have something in common with other participants. Eventually they feel confident enough to pick a person at the lunch table to sit next to, or send a chat in an online session.

We can help our teens notice the little steps that bring about different results than they had had with their limiting belief.

Step 4: Introduce new beliefs. Once we've challenged a limiting belief and exposed it as untrue and disempowering, what does the "new" belief look like? It's key to *identify* and *name* the new belief to give the brain something exciting to build new neural pathways around.

Back to the example of the teen who didn't believe she was good at making friends: She might say, *I am great at making friends. I am a good, caring, loyal friend to my friends*, and other affirming statements that allow her to step into the new belief. Her small steps grow into bigger ones, like holding an online party or joining a club to meet new people.

I encourage teens to turn negative opinions into good ones which support their new belief. They begin to carry themselves with more confidence. They notice their actions change for the better, as do the results they receive.

Beliefs are personal

At this point in the process, I remind my teens that a belief is something they can CHOOSE TO ACCEPT because it empowers them—or NOT CHOOSE because it limits them.

A tip for parents: Don't "tell" your teen what new beliefs should replace the old, limiting ones, however obvious it might be. It's not for us to decide.

In one group coaching call, I presented teens with a set of beliefs and led a conversation on each, reminding the kids these were beliefs, not facts. They could choose to keep the belief if it empowered, or throw it away if it limited.

What followed was a fascinating conversation where we looked objectively at different interpretations of the beliefs presented. Some kids saw a "new" belief that could help them, such as the freedom to see mistakes as opportunities to learn, rather than to regret or self-judge, while others didn't feel that same way and shared why.

I myself learned from these teens some new ways of thinking about the beliefs I presented! We adults can be so sure that our own life experiences, knowledge, and beliefs will empower the teens we work or live with. However, we can do teens a disservice by assuming *our* beliefs are empowering to *them*.

A teen who excelled in sports once shared with the group about the time she was injured, lying in a hospital bed with an epidural in her back. Her mom was at her side encouraging her to "keep pushing and keep going." Is it possible that this teen and her mom were not on the same page in terms of beliefs?

How to help your teen work with their limiting beliefs

1. Recognize any belief that keeps your teen from unlocking their potential as a limiting belief. Assure your teen that beliefs are not always facts, and they *have the power* to change their thoughts. Keep the beliefs that are empowering and supportive. Release the others.

2. Challenge the limiting belief by asking two key questions: *Why does this have to be true? What evidence do you have that it's true?* Help your teen break down the elements of the belief with questions that let them see *for themselves* whether or not the belief is true and empowering.

3. Encourage the concept that beliefs affect actions and results. Whether limiting or empowering, beliefs WILL influence our actions and, subsequently, our results. Explore if a belief is bringing your teen what they want. If not, they have a choice to go for what feels good and right and brings them more happiness.

4. Avoid "telling" your teen what new beliefs should replace the old, limiting ones. It's not for us to decide, however obvious it might be. It's more powerful and lasting when teens make these discoveries on their own. Help them explore beliefs and let them choose what they are going to keep believing.

SECTION II

Understanding and Living With Emotions

CHAPTER 4

Feelings, Emotions, Moods, and Perceptions

Any adult who has spent time with a teenager knows emotions and feelings figure BIG into the adolescent experience. Hormones are raging, school pressures are increasing, exciting and challenging experiences pop up every day.

I've noticed in my work that teens definitely know they have emotions, and many would like to control them. What's new for them is diving deeper into what's BEHIND their emotions. There's a lot of judgment and confusion around "good" feelings, "bad" feelings, what's "acceptable" and what is not, which help lead to the limiting beliefs we talked about in Chapter 3.

> *"Feelings are much like waves. You cannot stop them from*
> *coming but you can decide which ones to surf."*
> —*Jonatan Martensson*

Couldn't agree more! In a recent group coaching call, I talked teens through a game I call "Time Jumping," to help them get in touch with their emotions and show they have the control to access them:

Teen Talk

Dr. RJ: Here is a bagful of emotions and guess what? You don't have to ask for it or pay for it. You literally open your bag, grab any emotion you want and there you are! Don't believe me? Then let's do some Time Jumping: Think about the last time you were laughing so hard you snorted. Think about that situation. Everybody got theirs?

[Teens respond in online chat space]

> Great! Now, jump to that time and RELIVE it. Replay it in your head. Where were you? Who was there? Feel what you experienced in that laughing moment.
>
> What are you feeling right now? Happy, right? Maybe even laughing again at just the thought of that moment. Well, you just grabbed a great emotion out of your bag. You have access to any emotion you want, at any time. The more you practice the emotions that make you feel good and confident, the more you are rewiring your brain.

Feelings and emotions—what's the difference?

Feelings are not the same as emotions, and this is an important distinction for teens to make. An emotion describes what is happening to our body. For example, if we looked out our door and saw a huge bear, we'd be terrified—that's an emotion. What happens to our body is triggered by the amygdala, the "fight-flight-or-freeze" part of our brain. The blood flow increases, our hearts beat faster. We breathe faster and shallower. Our faces flush and feel hot, we feel shaky, and we might start to sweat.

A feeling is the conscious experience of the emotional reaction. ***Feelings are how we describe emotions***. In short, feelings are mental associations, whereas emotions are physical responses. After using the terrifying bear example, I then describe another situation to my teens: *Say you have a crush on someone, and you decide to go up to talk to them for the first time. What emotion are you experiencing?* Of course, they describe almost the exact same body messages—heart pounding, sweating, shaking, face feeling hot and flushed.

Are you terrified like you were with the bear? Well, no, maybe more like nervous or excited. What we discover together is our body doesn't know the difference, but our mind does. We have the superpower of analysis and discernment!

This is an important distinction for teens to understand for two reasons:

They gain a more objective perspective on what feelings and emotions are. Different people will have different feelings in response to the same situation.

The feeling of a pounding heart and shortness of breath is interpreted as terror when faced with a bear, but interpreted as excitement when asking your crush on a date. Same emotion, two different feelings.

Teens are empowered when they see their emotions are not EVERY-THING. Their minds are in the driver's seat, not their emotions!

Learning how one's body reacts to internal and external situations helps a teen identify what's happening to them. They can use this information to assess if they're physically and emotionally okay. (I talk more about this in Chapter 5 on depression.)

Teens learn that emotions are a message from the body, and feelings give them a message too—it's their job.

"You know you're feeling an emotion because you're feeling it in your body," says Joie Seldon, author of *EMOTIONS: An Owners Manual*.[11] "Emotions are an information system that is physiological, meaning body-based...Each emotion has an inherent message which is conveyed through your body in order to move you either away from danger or towards pleasure and fulfillment."

Go back to the Thought Triangle: The way teens think about the body's messages influences their actions which lead to a result, "good" or "bad." The gold nugget is teens can at least choose the *potential* for a good result.

So how does a teen hop in the driver's seat when it comes to their feelings and emotions? ***Pay attention!*** Note what's going on in their body when a feeling shows up. Watch for the messages and the emotion(s) they're experiencing.

If a teen is with friends, laughing, joking, playing video games, or listening to music, their body is giving them the message that they are feeling good. They want more of that, and the good news is that they can "Time Jump" to that emotion of happiness, contentment, joy, etc., any time they want.

If a teen feels "bad" about something, they can tap into the thoughts contributing to the feeling and the emotion behind it. I suggest they say to themselves, *"Thank you for the message. I understand that my thoughts are contributing to the way I feel right now. I will change my thoughts so that I can get a better result."*

This is an empowering lesson for teens. In fact, it's an important reminder for people of all ages. You can choose what you invite and spend time with. Feelings and emotions are important, but they are NOT permanent.

---

[11] https://joieseldon.com

Perception: What is your favorite P-Lens?

When feelings, emotions, and hormones bump up against each other, the result becomes what we call "moods." I don't have to tell you that teenage moods can go up and down like a roller coaster—one minute they are happy and excited, the next they are angry or annoyed!

Moods are a new experience for teens, and I find they often aren't sure what to do when their moods feel so out of control. (Note to parents: Your teen probably doesn't want those frustrating moods any more than you do!) Teens sometimes ask me, *how do I maintain happy thoughts?* Or, *how do I keep my moods from going wild?*

I tell them about the P-lens. The "P" stands for *perception.*

These days, if you don't like your eye color, you can buy colored contact lenses. You can find sunglasses with lenses in almost every color, and they'll give the world a different hue when you look through them.

P-lenses don't improve one's vision, but they can definitely change it. The job of the P-lens is to interpret the events of your life.

Just like contact lenses come in different colors, P-lenses come in a variety of emotions such as anger, fear, happiness, sadness, hope and despair. Whichever lens you choose determines your mood, which determines your actions, and we already know how actions lead to results—those that we want as well as those we don't.

If a teen says, *Man, I sure got up on the wrong side of the bed today,* they might have had a morning like this: They slept through their alarm, and their mother came into the room, "screaming" they were going to be late. They threw on their clothes, ran a comb through their hair, and stormed out of the house. Halfway down the street, they realized they forgot their school project and house keys, and had to run back to get them. They arrived at school just after the bell, huffing and puffing and disheveled.

What type of P-lens is the teen wearing when they sit down in their first class? You can bet their outlook is stressed, disoriented, distracted, and angry. If they're not aware of the P-lens they're wearing in this moment, they could spend the entire day in the same mood, only seeing things that continue to make their day awful.

Default Lenses: Why is it important to choose the P-lens you want to wear?

Our default P-lens is our natural reaction to a given situation, based on our personality, past experiences, and beliefs. If you are aggressive by nature, then your default lens would tend to be angry, confrontational, aggravated, or annoyed. If you are extremely passive by nature, your default lens would lean toward being sad, offended, defeated, or fearful. If you tend toward optimism, your default P-lens would be positive, upbeat, cheerful, and playful.

Here are some examples that came up in one of our teen group coaching discussions:

TEEN TALK

Dr. RJ: There are times when your default P-lens can help you, but many times it can stand in the way of your happiness. Let's look at two stories that show how different P-lenses might interpret the exact same situation.

"Joey" hears that her classmates were laughing at her story on social media. Because she sees the world through a P-lens of low self-esteem and self-doubt, she instantly feels like everyone in the school is laughing at her. She rushes to the restroom and cries, believing no one likes her, and she'll always be laughed at. She is sad all day and avoids others, even the friends who reach out to do something with her after school.

"Antoine" hears that his classmates were laughing at his story on social media. Knowing he's a person who can choose his P-lens, he feels hurt at first, but then he laughs it off. Later, he makes up another embarrassing story, but this time makes it even funnier.

Let's talk about which result you would rather have and how you can work with your default P-lens.

The only way for the teen to prevent themselves from wearing their default P-lens all the time is to actively choose the type of P-lens they want to wear—and there are as many to choose from as there are colors. It's great practice for a teen to experiment with their P-lens and take control of their roller-coaster moods.

I offer my teens these steps to choose P-lenses that help build a healthy, positive perception of the world. I invite parents and adults who work with teens to support this practice too.

Ask yourself: "What is my favorite P-lens?" If happiness is your favorite lens, then whenever you wake up in the morning—even before you brush your teeth—put on your happiness lens.

Tell yourself: "No matter what happens today, I will be happy." The easiest way to be happy is to just smile—and you do not need a reason for it! Just smile! (You know it's my favorite thing!) If laughter is your favorite lens, then choose to laugh all day. Look for things that are funny. Tell jokes. Look at social media sites that have funny stories and videos.

Try on your favorite P-lens for a week and observe your feelings, emotions, and moods. I bet you'll see some differences, in a good way.

Of course, just like all the colors of lenses, **you may choose different lenses for different situations**. Maybe at lunch your favorite P-lens is the "silly" one. In a sport, your favorite lens could be "determined." When you're with your younger sibling, your favorite lens could be "caring."

My favorite P-lens at work is my "excitement" lens. I love my job so it's easy for me to wear it. My favorite lenses at home with my family are the "fun" and "loving" ones. When I'm at the gym, I wear my "inspiration" lens. One's P-lenses can be anything they want them to be, *as long as the person feels good wearing them and they cause no harm to themselves or others.*

We want to be aware that our default P-lens comes from survival thinking (thanks to the amygdala) and if we are not mindful, it can run the show and create an unbalanced and out-of-control experience. Our goal is for our teens to make good choices for themselves rather than always wearing a default pair that has them feeling sad, "not enough," or holds them back from going for their dreams.

The message for our teens: By choosing your P-lenses, not only are you creating a great day, you're building your perception of the world—one that will empower you to do wonderful, exciting things.

How to help your teen develop a healthy relationship with their emotions

1. Help them practice getting in touch with their emotions. If you're at dinner, or in the car, or hanging out in the evening, the Time Jumping game can be a fun and easy way to engage. You can also call attention to your own feelings and emotions during an experience, such as: *This ice cream is so yummy and creamy. Look at the sky and all the stars. I'm glad we came to this ice cream shop. I feel really happy and peaceful right now. How do you feel?*

2. Listen to the messages that feelings and emotions offer. During adolescence, teenagers are extremely interested in (and sometimes scared of) their bodies. Help your teen practice awareness of their feelings and the messages their body gives them, such as: *That car almost hit us—wow, that was a close call. Was that scary? My heart is still racing and I'm sweaty! You too?*

3. Choose their favorite P-lenses. The job of the P-lens is to interpret the events of one's life. If events are always interpreted through a pessimistic lens, then a teen will build neuropathways to support pessimism and fear. We can teach our teens that their brains and thoughts are not fixed in stone. Instead, they have a choice in how to perceive a moment, a situation, and their whole day.

CHAPTER 5

Living Day-to-Day With Emotions

Once teens understand what is behind their feelings, emotions, and perceptions—and that they have control over all of it through their thoughts and choices—they have the foundation of some really important knowledge to leverage their experience of adolescence. But then.... they're unleashed into the wild, everyday world of Real Life!

It can get complicated.

It's one thing to notice, understand, and "get" the science of feelings and emotions. It's another thing to self-regulate those feelings and emotions to cope with all the various encounters and new experiences that a teenager will face every single day. We adults have had a lot of experience with coping in different situations, so it's easy to forget how new all this is to our teens. We may wonder why they're overreacting to some of the simplest things. We might even get impatient or angry about it.

I'm with you on that—sometimes those reactions are justified. Our teens need the boundaries we set for appropriate behavior with their fellow humans, and boundaries for self-behavior. When they get out of control or act inappropriately, we need to rein them in.

At the same time, we want to remember that teens' egos can be fragile. The fight-or-flight part of their brain is ruling over common sense, and hormones are causing their emotions to run rampant!

Managing emotions is a subject I often talk to my teens about because, as I mentioned earlier, they KNOW all this craziness is happening, and they really want to learn what to do with all the emotions and moods. Here are a few insights and techniques I offer to them.

How to put the brakes on your ego and take control of your emotions

When we make decisions we regret later, what is happening in those moments? How do we get to that place of regret?

In almost every case teens share with me, regret happens when the ego steps in to "protect," and crowds out any clear thinking about a situation. Something occurs that a teen sees as unfair or mean, such as a friend who forgets to text them, a teacher who gives them a lower grade than expected, the cheerleading coach doesn't put them on the team, or a parent has them do chores they don't want to do.

"Unfair" or "mean" are common emotional triggers for teens because they have one foot in the world they remember from childhood (*it's all about me*), and another foot in the new world of diversity, attitudes, interpretations, and perceptions. The ego is always ready to step up, indignant and affronted and mad—how dare you do that TO ME!

Later we'll get into the emotions that are triggered the most often in these situations, but first, let's get to the root of WHY this happens, and what a teenager needs to know about responding in ways they can be proud of instead of regretting.

Like the P-Lens (perception), the ego is how a person chooses to interpret the events of their life. "[The ego] is a trickster; it's the chatter that avoids all responsibility and blames others. It's the chatter that makes you a poor victim," says Stella Grizont, writing for *Forbes*.[12] I teach my teens that they are MORE than their ego. The ego is just one part of their personality, and when it gets louder, it's usually because it's "speaking" mostly from fear.

"One of the most deceptive aspects of the ego is that it generates powerful emotional reactions and then blames us for how it made us feel."[13] Talk about unfair!

The first thing to help the teen understand is the destructive effect of the ego. Have them talk about a situation where they did or said something they

---

[12] https://www.forbes.com/sites/forbescoachescouncil/2018/01/05/three-ways-to-control-your-ego-and-stop -thinking-so-much-without-having-to-meditate/?sh=686808556f2e
[13] https://pathwaytohappiness.com/blog/what-is-the-ego/

regretted later. Most often, the driver of their reaction was the ego. In my teen sessions, I help them take apart the situation through the power of their thoughts and positive P-lens. Nine times out of ten, they realize they sabotaged themselves with their response.

This is "Tony's" experience that came up in the online teen group coaching session:

TEEN TALK

Dr. RJ: Someone give me a real-life example of the last time you were extremely upset.

Tony: My mom said my curfew was at 11:30 when we already agreed to 12:30. I was really mad because she changed it when I was already out with my friends! I was mad and my mom just doesn't get it. She doesn't like me. I don't like her. She's so unfair.

Dr. RJ: There are a lot of ways you might react. It's predictable to get angry and maybe yell (which NEVER would have happened in my mom's house—I was never brave enough to do that!). Maybe you purposely do something to get back at your parents, like, *I'm just not going to study; I'm going to get an F in English, then she'll get it.* Or you might just ignore what she says and stay out until 12:00 or even later.

What do you think your parents' reaction will be?

Tony: I'll probably get locked-down grounded. The relationship with my mom will be even worse.

Dr. RJ: Can you see how you sabotage yourself and your own success with your ego-driven reaction?

Tony: Yeah.

Dr. RJ: I'm curious, Tony, why do you think your mom changed your curfew?

Tony: I figured she forgot. I texted her that my curfew was 12:30. I came home, gave her a kiss, and went to bed. She called me down, which I figured she would. And she said that my curfew was 11:30. But if my dad agreed, it would be 12:00. So I just decided to take it for what it was. Twelve isn't so bad. I figured she would say something like that. So I'm not really stressed. And everything was good the next morning.

Dr. RJ: Oh, Tony, give me some virtual high fives—that's what I'm talking about! THIS is the way to show your ego who's driving the car!

Tony was a student who'd been on my calls for a while, learning the concepts I'm sharing in this book. He was able to be present in his situation and understand his mom had one interpretation, and he had another interpretation. He decided in the moment that his mom didn't hate him, she wasn't just trying to be mean, she didn't do this on purpose to embarrass him in front of his friends—she just forgot. No big deal. He chose not to get angry, not to storm in the house with his ego ready for a fight.

He made a positive interpretation of the situation, and everything worked out well. Was his relationship better with his mom? We don't know, but we do know he didn't escalate the situation to drive them further apart, and he got what he wanted in the end. I was SO proud of him for seeing the situation, knowing his ego could have gone wild, yet he thought reasonably and chose a reaction that was positive and responsible.

Now, I'm not telling or expecting teenagers to be emotionless or to choose to concede to the other person all the time. It's impossible to be emotionless. It's natural for teens to get sad or frustrated if parents tell them something they don't like.

What I ask is for them to go to a "higher level" to get what they want and to feel happy. This means going beyond the ego, the limiting beliefs, the self-talk that tears teens down. We want kids to develop the ability to maintain a higher level of emotion—happiness, excitement, gratitude, love, peace, inspiration.

Suppose I make a comment within a group of people and a friend says, *That's the dumbest thing I've ever heard!* It hurts, I feel bad. At this point I have a choice: I know my emotions are giving me a message: *I don't like how it felt when she said that.* That's what I'm feeling and it's real to me. I have the choice then to reset, PAY ATTENTION to my feelings and emotions, and consider my interpretation.

I can choose to think it wasn't about me, wonder if maybe she's having a bad day, she wasn't trying to hurt my feelings but just reacting without thinking. Whatever the reason, I'm not going to take it personally.

This process may happen in a few moments or may take a few days or a week—that's okay, this is new to the teen. However long it takes, the process of attention and analysis will show them they have power over their thoughts and reactions. By not giving into whatever emotion pops up, they come out of the situation feeling better about themselves. ***The ultimate benefit of this practice is immeasurable because it shows teenagers how to fully love themselves.***

Do you allow disappointment to be disappointing?

Disappointment is another emotional trap for teenagers. For all the developmental reasons we've talked about, teens feel emotions deeply and their moods can shift drastically. Their childhood world is no longer simple. "Good" stuff happens, and "bad" stuff happens. "Success" happens and so does "failure." This means lots of potential disappointments. Sometimes their team loses, they don't get the grades they expected, an uncomfortable change in the family happens, a trusted friend turns against them. It's important for teens to learn how to handle these events.

In his article[14], clinical psychologist David Bakker describes signs of disappointment to look for in your teen:

- They've indicated they feel let down.
- They've become withdrawn or pessimistic.
- They're upset things aren't perfect.
- They're using more drugs or alcohol than usual.

He goes on to suggest to parents that "how you respond to your child's disappointment will influence how they learn to deal with obstacles." Here are some ways to help your teen process their feelings:

- Encourage them to acknowledge their emotions.
- Reassure them that they can talk to you about them.
- Teach them how to put events in a larger context, so that they can see things in perspective.

---

[14] https://parents.au.reachout.com/common-concerns/everyday-issues/things-to-try-single-parenting-and-teenagers/talking-to-your-teen-about-disappointment

I work with teens on managing disappointment by understanding what "disappointment" is and what we can choose to do with it (you figured out that I love the power of choice!). Sometimes life just doesn't work out the way we want it to, and we immediately experience disappointment. It can feel as though we've been punched in the stomach.

Thankfully, ***disappointment is just another emotion in the magic grab bag***, which means it can be let go just as fast as it got picked up. Feelings and emotions are designed to give us a message, and we can invite them to LEAVE when their job is done.

The problem is many teens *hold onto* emotion. Hence, the disappointment becomes devastating and the cycle can go on for hours, days or months. When they hold onto disappointment, they are positioning themselves for a lifelong, unhealthy perspective on goals and success.

Again, it's important for teens not to ignore emotions or push bad feelings away. We shouldn't "shield our children from pain or sadness [or] we run the risk of diminishing their emotional depths," according to the Center for Parent & Teen Communication.[15] The best parents can do is to support their teen, as Dr. Bakker suggests, by encouraging them to talk about and process their emotions and then move on, rather than go down any black hole of emotional self-harm.

The "moving on" part can be sticky. Once they've acknowledged the feelings of disappointment, I offer my teens a process to diffuse the emotion and invite disappointment to leave.

Three ways to process disappointment

1. Stay in the present. When something doesn't go your way, you immediately go down the slippery slope of "the future." You not only give yourself magical powers to predict the future, you create a future that doesn't exist yet. You continue a disappointing story by giving it a disappointing ending. Sounds like an unproductive cycle, doesn't it?

---

[15] https://parentandteen.com/support-teens-release-emotions/

For example, you don't get the grade you thought you deserved on a major science project. You feel disappointment, possibly anger, shame, frustration, and a host of other natural reactions. While processing all these emotions, you Time Jump into an imaginary future: *All the kids in my class are going to make fun of me. I'll never pass a science test again. Nothing ever works out right. I'm going to keep on being a failure and bad things will keep happening to me.*

The thing to do is stay in the present moment! Accept the emotion of disappointment, allow the other emotions to wash over you, give you their message. Then tell them thanks and GOODBYE! With clarity and calm, you can make the decision to persevere and move on, knowing this disappointing event will have little to no effect on your overall destination.

2. Talk about it. I find it takes longer to overcome disappointment when you deal with it alone. Remember, it's normal to experience disappointment. Everyone experiences disappointment. Talking about it with others gives you an opportunity to vent. When you share your feelings aloud, it can feel like a weight being lifted from your shoulders. ***When you verbally share your feelings, you no longer have to keep them inside.*** Be sure to choose a trusted friend, mentor, or parent who will listen, support, and love you through it.

3. Take action! The easiest way to get over disappointment is to take action toward your goals. Look at it like a road trip—your goal is the destination. An emotion will alert you to changing road conditions, and you can decide to stay the course or take a detour. Whichever decision you make, act as soon as possible. Why? ***It is almost impossible to take action toward a goal and be disappointed at the same time—the two just don't mix.*** Therefore, act quickly, so disappointment won't steal time away from you.

It doesn't have to be a huge action or one that gives immediate results. Just take one step toward a goal, any goal. Let's say your main goal is try out for the soccer team, and your feelings aren't quite up to practicing your dribbling skills. No problem! It's the movement of action that helps disappointment to disappear. Go ahead and make progress towards another goal such as finishing reading a novel or learning a new trick on your skateboard.

Your mind needs to make progress to feel good. With movement and action, you give your mind, your energy, and your mood a big gift, and you won't be disappointed by your disappointment anymore!

Handling disappointments is of developmental importance

I really want to emphasize how ***understanding disappointment is an important aspect of the growth process*** is so important. The understanding determines how well the teen will handle disappointment, expectations, and ambition as an adult.

"The way we handle disappointments is related to our developmental history—our relationship with our parents and other early, formative experiences," says Manfred F.R. Kets de Vries, writing for the *Harvard Business Review*.[16] A person who wants to avoid disappointment may turn into an underachiever, so they "unconsciously set the bar low and avoid taking risks, to prevent themselves or others from being disappointed." I think we can safely say that they end up disappointing themselves the most.

At the other end of the spectrum are people who have grown up with high expectations of perfection, putting extreme pressure on themselves. They become overachievers and set bars unrealistically high. This also leads to disappointment with themselves, because they make their expectations impossible to meet.

The best result is teenagers achieving a healthy balance between the two extremes. Name disappointment, teach what it is and what it looks like, and encourage teens to feel the emotions around disappointment. Then, process and let go. (In Section IV I'll go into greater depth on goals, motivation, success, and happiness, as well as contributors to a balanced perspective.)

How to help your teen understand and manage emotions in daily life

1. Recognize when the ego is taking control. Ego mostly speaks from fear, which is an emotion that can really hold a teen back. Indicators that the ego has stepped in are the words "unfair" and "mean" (by the way, it isn't helpful to respond with *life's not fair*—that's a surefire confidence buster!). Encourage

---

[16] https://hbr.org/2018/08/dealing-with-disappointment

your teen not to blame someone else for their interpretation of what happened. Support them in taking apart the situation. Identify the response that will get what they want, as opposed to a reaction they'll regret later. Teens are amazing! When they're given the support and space to explore in this way, they figure it out themselves.

2. Watch for signs that your teen is experiencing disappointment. Disappointment may not seem like a big emotion to adults, but it is a BIG deal for teenagers! They're experiencing so many new aspects of life that they never did in childhood. "Failure"—mistakes, breakups, losing—can be devastating, and their reactions extreme. *Here are the signs to look for: feeling let down; becoming withdrawn or pessimistic; upset that things aren't perfect; using more drugs or alcohol than usual (or other self-harming behaviors).*

3. Handling disappointment well leads to facing all obstacles well. Support your teen when they show disappointment. Encourage them to acknowledge feelings and emotions, help them see the bigger picture. This leads to a more positive P-lens and sets them back on course with positivity, motivation, and hope.

4. Support them in working through disappointment. 1. Encourage them to stay present with their emotions and not Time Jump to the future, imagining all the possible terrible outcomes. 2. Encourage them to talk it out with you or another person they trust. 3. Get them to do something productive, taking forward-moving action. Get them out of the house to do something they love, simple and small as it might be.

CHAPTER 6

When Emotions Take Over Your Life

Even with positive influence and guidance from the best of parents and mentors, life's challenges can overwhelm teenagers in deep, destructive ways. Being left alone with thoughts and emotions they don't understand is a tough situation for a teen.

In this chapter, I highlight some of the most common and difficult emotions that can overwhelm a teen: ***anxiety, anger, and depression.***

Anxiety

Anxiety is one of the most common issues teenagers face today. According to the National Institute of Mental Health (NIMH), almost 32% of adolescents aged 13-18 had an anxiety disorder. And percentages have steadily risen since this 2017 study.[17]

Many parents believe the reason teens suffer from anxiety is because of pressure. There are plenty of reasons to believe this, among them:

1. In a culture that values ***high achievement and competition*** for college, teens can feel intense pressure to succeed in school. Whether or not they plan to go on to college, the sense of pressure has a ripple effect throughout the school, the teachers, and the parents. Add online schooling during the pandemic and post-pandemic adjustments, and anxiety rises even more.

2. Kids are ***constantly connected to social media***, and today's teens have known nothing other than having several devices all "shouting" at them at once. With the bombardment of society's messages, advertising, and peer pressure, it's hard for them NOT to compare and judge themselves. The result is pressure to be smart, cool, beautiful, hot, fit, skinny, stylish, and on and on.

---

[17] https://www.nimh.nih.gov/health/statistics/any-anxiety-disorder.shtml#part_155096

3. ***The world can feel scary and uncertain***. Many teenagers experience drills and lockdowns in their schools to prepare them for shootings. Economic struggles and uncertainty add to the pressure to perform, and raise anxiety.

These are very real stressors, and parents/mentors are right to be concerned. It's important to address teen anxiety sooner rather than later. In my experience as a life coach, it often takes six to eight coaching sessions to help a teen overcome severe anxiety.

While external pressures can enhance symptoms of anxiety, stress, and worry, they are not the cause. The reason teenagers (even high-performing ones) suffer from anxiety is FEAR.

I talked about "emotion regulation skills" in Chapter 2, how teens are in the developmental stage of learning to process their thoughts, feelings, and emotions on a neurological level. The brain is also developing in other ways—specifically within the prefrontal cortex, whose function includes "complex cognitive behavior, personality expression, decision making, and moderating social behavior... Executive function relates to abilities to differentiate among *conflicting thoughts, determine good and bad, better and best, same and different, future consequences of current activities*" and more [italics added].[18]

The amygdala, the part of the brain that governs survival response (fight-flight-or-freeze) starts to develop at birth and still rules the roost in the teen's life. They haven't yet mastered how to respond reasonably to new, unfamiliar, and challenging things, and their "executive function" abilities are not yet developed.

If something feels threatening or dangerous, a teen's survival response is activated and it takes longer for the thinking part of their brain to process and evaluate the situation. ***The fear can become so strong and overwhelming, the teen can't think themselves out of it.***

Without a fully developed cortex (which doesn't happen until their early-to mid-twenties!), the teen can get stuck in fear. They often go down a rabbit hole of "fear thinking," imagining the worst in a situation.

Studying for a big test, given the "adult" responsibility of an important errand, playing in a championship game, going on a first date, learning a friend's parent died of cancer—all these situations can seem frightening. The

---

[18] https://www.thescienceofpsychotherapy.com/prefrontal-cortex/

fear shows up as worry, pressure, tension, anxiety, and more, and can lead to obsessive thinking and panic attacks, or more serious disorders.

What's behind the pressure?

It's important to work with what's BEHIND the worry, pressure, and tension you see in your teenager. ***Removing the pressure isn't going to remove the fear.*** There are many personality-based tools I use to help teens overcome anxiety. I want to share one of my favorite exercises that helps the teen face fears by exploring worst-case scenarios.

I call it the "Rabbit Hole Game." The goal is to help the teen experience different worst-case scenarios in their mind. Then, as a team, we identify the obstacles and create scenarios to overcome those obstacles and achieve the desired goal that triggered the fear in the first place.

"Maynard," an 18-year-old who wanted to be a surgeon, ranked #2 in his class at a very competitive high school, scoring in the top percentile on the PSAT. So why was he fearful, anxious, and having panic attacks? In my experience, the more success teenagers experience, the more they feel they have to lose. Here's how we used the Rabbit Hole Game in our sessions:

Teen Talk

Dr. RJ: Maynard, share with me your worst-case scenario.

Maynard: I will score a 90 on the exam and then I will lose my confidence and continue to score below a 97 after that. I will not graduate at the top of my class. I'll take the SAT and fall to the 88th percentile which means I will not get into my first college choice.

Then my grades in college will not be the best since I lost my confidence, and I will not do well on the MCAT. Therefore, I will have to settle for another career in which I'm sure I will be miserable.

Dr. RJ: Wow, it makes sense you'd be fearful! If you scored a 90 on your exam, what could you do to gain your confidence back?

If you scored below a 97 on the next three exams, what could you do to still graduate at the top of your class?

If you scored in the 88th percentile on your SAT, what could you do to still get accepted into your top college?

If your grades in college were not the best, what could you do to perform well on the MCAT?

If you did not do well on the MCAT, what could you do to get accepted into medical school?

If you do not get accepted into medical school on your first try, what could you do to pursue your dream of becoming a surgeon?

We went over Maynard's answers one by one. We kept going down the "rabbit hole" until Maynard's imagination started to come back to reality. For each worst-case scenario, we created a new scenario to overcome the obstacles he felt he was facing. He was able to recognize his worst fears were not realistic, and there were multiple paths he could take to achieve his goals (and happiness).

This process needs to be taken slowly, patiently, and with lots of loving support. Fears start early in a child's life and develop in one form or another into adolescence. Teens are smart—they can come up with all kinds of rationalizations about why their anxiety is real. But they're also smart and resourceful enough to create great solutions to get rid of their fears.

A certified life coach is a good choice to help a teen through this process of discovery, because some very deep things can come up and often the teen doesn't want to share these fears with their parents. However, sometimes a parent can give a teen the safe space to talk about their fears by simply asking curious questions and listening to the answers. When a teen states their fear out loud, it dampens fear's power. They see for themselves which worst-case scenarios are silly once they've talked them out—so they can let go of them. It's key not to judge. Just listen and love.

Anger

I want everyone to be happy. One of the things holding teens back from happiness is anger. We all get angry and we do use anger for certain, positive purposes: I might use anger to make me run faster, to act when I see a social injustice happening, or to step in when I see someone being bullied.

However, it's important for teens to understand two things: 1) anger is not their friend if they don't know how to handle or diffuse it; and 2) when anger shows up, it shouldn't be allowed to hang around a week, a month, or even years.

Many of us have gotten angry about something that happened all the way back in childhood, and if we're not careful, we can carry it until the day we die. I like to let teens know this applies to me, them, their parents, all the adults in their life. We're all human, we all have emotions, and some of us struggle hard with anger. The sooner we become aware of and work through situations that trigger our anger, the happier we will become!

When I ask teens what makes them angry, here are some answers I get:

I don't get straight A's. I mean, I just don't study. I promise myself I'll do better, then I don't.

The bossy cheerleaders. I didn't make the varsity cheerleading team. It's not fair.

Stress. I have a sharp temper. I'm angry at myself, my parents, my homework.

When I don't do what my mom wants me to, she takes away my phone. It never works when she does that so I wish she would do something else."

My boyfriend cheated on me.

So when I get in trouble sometimes and my parents get mad at me, I take it really deep and get angry at myself and think of everything I did wrong. It's like my fault.

Here comes that EGO again...

Anger is a place where the ego rears its protective head in unhelpful ways.

How many teens (and adults—come on, you know you've done it! I'm guilty too!) play this game: You're mad at a friend. You react by avoiding them.

They know you're mad but they don't ask about it. And you don't go to them. You just wait it out expecting your friend to come to you and apologize. This goes on for who-knows-how long.

Does this strategy work? No! It would be much faster to go to the friend and say, *Listen, what you did the other day really upset me.* (I get into this more in the chapters on relationships and communication.) But why don't we do that? Because our ego is protecting us. It doesn't want us to put ourselves out there. It thinks we don't want to be vulnerable, we don't want to be hurt. The ego "protects" us and that's where anger comes from.

Anger becomes destructive when we don't deal it and keep holding onto it. We stay mad about something that happened a week ago or even decades ago, thinking about it but never resolving it.

Of course, it all comes back to our thoughts: **What we *think about is what we feel and focus on.*** I want teens to ask themselves: *Is hanging onto this anger helping me or holding me back?*

Anger often flares up when a teen is faced with new situations they don't have the experience to handle—which, at this stage in their development, is often! With all that's going on around and inside them, they need practical techniques to blow off the steam that builds up inside like a pressure cooker.

The Anger Reset Exercise

I walk my teens through three steps that move them out of the angry moment and toward a "reset," before they make stupid decisions they'll definitely regret later.

Anger in the moment is one thing, but you don't want it to last for too long, in a way that hurts you. When teens find a way to quickly shift their energy, they can release the anger, the moment, and then look at the situation with the clear vision of the P-lens.

Here's how the Anger Reset Exercise goes:

Step one: BREATHE and release the anger. Breathing is the key to all life. Giving yourself oxygen will naturally start to calm you down and relieve your anxiety.

Take a deep breath to a steady count of six. Hold it for two counts (say one thousand one, one thousand two), then exhale for another steady count of six. Pause and do it again until you feel yourself getting calmer or your heart stops beating so fast.

You can do it quietly in the moment or take yourself away from the situation and do it privately. At the worst, wait until you are at home or another safe space.

Breathing intentionally and deeply resets your mind and calms your body.

Step two: MOVE. Real movement, like jumping up and down a few times, a ninja move, or any crazy movement you don't usually do. If possible, do it right in the moment, otherwise do it as soon as you can.

A quick, deliberate movement breaks up mental patterns. If you don't do this, then right after you breathe regularly again, your thoughts, emotions and ego will go straight back to the situation that triggered you.

Like well-programmed AI (artificial intelligence) your brain processes familiar patterns and repeats them when it gets familiar signals, like an "anger trigger." Abrupt movements block the trigger and prepare you for the next step.

Step three: CHANGE your perception. You're now calm and clear enough to choose a different-colored P-lens.

We know your ego is going to interrupt here: *Wait a minute, why do I have to change my perception? I'm mad so I'm just gonna sit in my room and stay mad!*

Ask your ego a simple question: *Why did my mom take my phone away? Why did my boyfriend cheat on me? Why did I accidentally forget to turn in my homework assignment again?*

The first answer you'll hear is the protective ego complaining how you were hurt or wronged by the situation, which of course will just rile you up and make you angry, panicky, sad all over again. Write the ego's answer down on a piece of paper—***then cross it off.***

Ask again and be ready for the ego's answers to keep making you feel angry or bad about yourself. ***These answers are false, so your job now is to challenge the responses, cross them off, and not give up!***

After a few of these exchanges, you'll begin to think of something that makes you feel better. Trust me—nine times out of ten, the reason which feels good is the true one, or at least one that makes sense.

With this knowledge, you can shift your thoughts like so:

He cheated on me because I'm not worthy shifts to *"it's clear we're not meant for each other.*

Mom takes away my phone because I'm a troublemaker shifts to *Mom literally doesn't have a strategy to encourage me. She just doesn't know what else to do.*

My friend ditched me because they hate me shifts to *maybe we do need a break, but I wish they would have communicated better.*

Powerful, isn't it? You're back in the superpower driver's seat again!

The Anger Reset Exercise is very effective in teaching teens to create a healthier relationship with the strong emotion of anger. However, a word of caution: A teen who is grappling with explosive anger that harms themselves or others may need professional help.

Depression

Teenagers are very aware of depression, much more than when I was growing up. I ask them why they think depression is more common now than in previous generations. Typical answers are: the internet, toxic people, access to more information and bad news, the pandemic. Pretty smart, right?

These days, the word "depression" is thrown around so commonly that I don't believe teens comprehend what it really means. In fact, some teens think it's cool to be depressed, and "depression" is just another part of teen life. This is not a positive thing!

We need to dig into what's BEHIND the term so teens know when or if they actually HAVE the clinical mental disorder called depression.

The difference between clinical depression and feeling depressed

According to the National Institute of Mental Health (NIMH): "Sadness is something we all experience. It is a normal reaction to a loss or a setback, but it usually passes with a little time. Depression is different." This statement is followed by a set of questions to ask to determine if a teen might have depression. Please visit the NIMH website to read the questions.[19]

While I'm not a clinical psychologist or psychiatrist, I am a certified teen life coach, and I'm ALWAYS in touch with the teens' parents about issues of mental health. I talk to my teens about depression from a place of thoughtfulness. I give them tips to shift their thoughts and energy when they feel sad or depressed about something.

My first goal is to help them realize there are two types of depression, so they don't use the term as a go-to for their feelings or, worse, so they don't ignore actual symptoms of depression and avoid doing anything until it's too late.

One type of depression is "clinical" depression. It is biological and out of a person's control, just like thyroid problems or diabetes. This type of depression is not the person's fault, and they need to see a doctor for treatment.

The other kind of depression is a feeling or emotion, usually about a sad situation, and maybe over a long period of time. The emotions described as "depression" are part of that "bag of emotions," not an illness. The emotions may feel serious and even debilitating, yet it is not a clinical depression. AND the good news is that they can do something about these emotions!

1. Our words inform our beliefs. Going back to the Thought Triangle, I remind teens that their thoughts drive their feelings and emotions, which drive their beliefs, actions, and results. If they know they don't have clinical depression, what happens to their beliefs if they still say, *I'm depressed*? They are creating or reinforcing a belief that isn't true, which just brings them more sadness.

2. Know the process of grief and sadness. I would never ask anyone to deny their feelings. Any teen who is going through grief—the loss of a pet, the death of their parent or close relative, a romantic breakup, going through the pandemic and all the loss they have experienced as a result—deserves respect, love, and support. I want teens to have knowledge of two things: 1) the difference between having depression and feeling depressed, and 2) these emotions are not permanent and teens have control over them. This knowledge gives the teen a kind of safety net to help them move through deep emotions when they arise, but not wallow in them.

---

[19] https://www.nimh.nih.gov/health/publications/teen-depression/index.shtml

3. Move your body! We remember how our body and mind are connected. When we're feeling sad, we don't want to do anything or see anyone. We don't feel inspired, we just want to stay home or even in bed with the covers pulled over our head. It's okay to feel like this for a little while. But the teen should know such behavior DOES NOT help them move through emotions and improve their mood. Instead, they need to get active! Jump up and down, dance, take a walk, run around the block, whatever will get their body moving so it will reduce cortisol (stress hormones) and release endorphins (happy hormones). Their emotions will flow through them, and they will naturally begin to feel better.

4. Expand your imagination and play. Imagination is an amazing gift. When we're feeling down, we often beat ourselves up with: *I have so much homework, but I'm not doing anything,* or *I'm supposed to practice but I just can't!* The idea is not to wallow and just do nothing. Instead, set those self-judgments aside, and do something fun and creative. Give yourself permission to just let go and imagine something amazing, something that makes you feel good. How could you sit in sadness if you are imagining something that's going to impact the entire world!

How to help your teen work through anxiety, anger, and depression

1. Anxiety: Guide them through their fears. Because the part of the brain that governs survival still rules the roost, teens feel pressure, stress, and anxiety that's rooted in FEAR. Support them in talking about their fears by asking curious questions and helping them explore the worst-case scenarios. They need to know our worst fears are almost never realized, and there are ALWAYS options for seemingly impossible situations. The Rabbit Hole exercise is probably best used by a professional who can facilitate the experience for the teen.

2. Anger: Let them know they are in control. 1) Anger is not their friend if they don't know how to handle it or diffuse it; 2) when anger comes up, it shouldn't be hanging around a week, a month or years. Knowing that anger is just another emotion in the bag empowers teens to control, diffuse, and deal with it.

3. Depression: Differentiate between clinical depression and feeling depressed. Support teens in exploring symptoms of depression to make sure they are diagnosed—something to do sooner than later! If they are not clinically depressed, help them identify and work through the exact emotions they're experiencing, without using the term "depression."

Relationships and Communication

CHAPTER 7

Who Is Your Teen Anyway?

I've spent A LOT of time with teens over the years, chatting with them in the orthodontist chair, coaching them one-on-one, hosting group sessions and in general, always honing my own P-lens (perceptions) so I can become a better coach. As a coach, my job is to be the teen's advocate (parents are always involved, though, and my teen clients know tit). I keep a safe space where they know they can tell me anything—and, believe me, they do!

Every teen is unique and awesome in their own special way, but all of them face similar challenges and pressures from society, school, peers, siblings, and parents. Parents (two parents, two sets of parents, one parent, a guardian) are often a big issue for teenagers.

If you're taking the time to read this book, then I know you are loving, caring, well-intentioned, and want happiness for your teen. I also know YOU know how difficult it can be to live with an adolescent. Kudos on taking it on every day!

When a parent becomes aware of how they come across to their kid, their eyes (P-Lens!) are opened in a new way. They begin to understand their own role in contributing to their teen's feelings of anger and angst. Once try something different, things become easier for EVERYBODY.

So would you like to know the kinds of things you might be doing that cause your teen to feel angry, upset, frustrated, "not enough," crushed or full of shame?

I thought so—let's do it!

What do teens wish their parents would stop doing?

Criticizing them. I couldn't explain it any better than this article, "5 Things Parents Do to Enrage Teenagers"[20]: "No one thrives in a critical environment. Constantly criticizing your kids makes them feel like failures...Teenagers may act tough, but underneath they have a very fragile sense of self. Golden rule: Never say anything to your kid that you wouldn't want someone to say to you."

Controlling them. Teens are sensitive to being treated "like children." Yes, I know they're still children in some ways, and sometimes act like toddlers in a tantrum, but *they* view themselves as adults through their P-lens. They're looking to you as a role model whether or not they're aware of it, or would admit it.

Within one household, teens are trying to live their lives and parents are trying to live theirs. The two lives don't always match. The battle for control is probably the toughest part of the teen-parent relationship.

Pressuring them to perform. While parents have the big-picture perspective of what it takes to excel, how competitive college admissions are, how much practice you need to "win," and so on, they don't always know or understand what it's like for the teen caught in the middle of all that. Most teens I talk to have a very clear idea of the pressures they're under: academic performance, responsibilities at home, peer pressure and cyberbullying, extra-curricular activities, drugs, vaping, teen depression stats, personal body image challenges, a world that feels uncertain and scary.

Remember the teen being treated with an epidural after a sports injury? She said, *I was lying on the table with an epidural in my back, so I couldn't move very well. Mom kept telling me to keep pushing and going.* This moment obviously affected her deeply, and her perception/interpretation was a mom who pressured her to excel in sports to the extreme. Even well-meaning parents can go too far in driving their kids to succeed.

---

[20] https://www.psychologytoday.com/us/blog/when-kids-call-the-shots/201802/5-things-parents-do-enrage-teenagers

What do teens wish their parents would do more?

Trust them. Here is a conversation with "Jannie" and her feelings about her mom. Jannie's parents were divorced, and she was living with her dad:

Teen Talk

Dr. RJ: Jannie, can you share an example of the time when you and your mom got into a big argument?

Jannie: Well, like whenever I'm at my dad's my mom asks me all the time what I'm doing. I'm like, you're not in charge of me right now. But she won't leave me alone, won't ever just leave me alone. I can't be my own person, ever. And she tries to be super overprotective, but I don't want that.

My dad trusts me to do stuff. My mom doesn't trust me—for no reason. I have to be at her house by 7:00 pm and I can't leave after I get there. I can't go out, can't see my friends. I know she wants the best for me, but it's annoying.

Understand they get stressed and anxious. When a parent keeps reminding their teen that the big test is on Friday, or this tournament game is the most important one they'll ever play, or the teen only has this year to build a resume for college apps...The teen wants to reply, *tell me something I don't know!* Remember teens spend 8-10 hours a day in the thick of expectations and pressures, and might need some positive acknowledgment of what they're going through.

Ask if they want advice. Sometimes a teen just wants their mom or dad to listen while the teen talks it out. When a teen decides to share, they often don't know what they need or what to ask for. So listen attentively and quietly, then ask: *Would you like me to share my thoughts?* Then accept their answer.

Let them form their own opinions, interests, and goals. Teens do want to share your interests and hear about your favorite music, goals, and dreams. But your favorites may not be their favorites. They want freedom to work through their own political or religious beliefs, their own interests and goals, their own preferences in arts, sports, and culture.

More truths about parent-teen relationships

Are you sitting down for this cold, hard truth?

No matter who you are and what you're like, at some point your teen will act like they just don't like you! It's their job. Adolescence is a time to separate from parents and find their own way in the world as an adult.

Whew, okay, we laid it right out there.

When your teen pushes back, ignores you, acts ashamed of you, and even says unacceptably rude things to you, it's not your fault! I'm here to give you peace of mind by saying I see this kind of thing *all the time.*

Generally speaking, what feels like a strained relationship with your teen is actually perfectly normal.

Psychologist Lisa Damour in her book, *Untangled: Guiding Teenage Girls through the Seven Transitions Into Adulthood,*[21] identifies seven tasks that teenagers are working on to move through adolescence to adulthood. ***Task #4 is "contending with adult authority."*** They notice things they hadn't in childhood and ask questions that might seem like pushing back or disrespectful, but what's behind it is part of their learning process.

And this is what we want for them—to begin to think for themselves. We want them to become adults who can evaluate authority figures, and make good decisions about who they want to trust, work with, and be in relationship with.

It's also the main reason why *Because I said so!* doesn't work anymore.

My best advice is to be patient, love them no matter what, support them where you can, and *be yourself.* Now, I'm not saying you should tolerate everything from them or be a doormat. It's your job as a parent, guardian, or mentor to be the authority figure in your teen's life, and believe me, they need that desperately in this confusing, ever-changing, and challenging world.

Being an authority figure doesn't mean being best friends. It means setting

---

[21] https://www.drlisadamour.com/untangled/

limits, boundaries, and a solid structure in your household that your children can count on and feel safe in.

Here are some pointers from Lisa Damour, and my added comments, on what parents/mentors/guardians can do:

Hold on loosely. Exerting more authority or control often leads to "outright rebellion or blind compliance"—neither would be in the teen's interests. You want to make sure your teen knows the rules and boundaries that are unquestionably meant to keep them safe, keep them on track at school, and cause no harm to themselves and others. At the same time, some expectations come across as micromanaging, which can look like you don't trust or respect your teen. Other expectations are about what *you* want, not what they really want. I'm not going to deny it's a balancing act!

Have clear expectations of your teen. Don't give up on trying to set rules. Teens need structure and boundaries. Clear expectations and rules are important to your teen, to your household—and to you. It's natural for teens to question or push against rules. Again, you're keeping them safe and on track, as well as showing them the benefits of authority.

Craft expectations that are both fair and flexible. Consistency gives teens a solid foundation while the figure out the crazy world they're living in (not to mention the adult world they're about to enter). If there are two parents, it's best if they try to be on the same page. A teen caught between two conflicting styles—one permissive, the other rigid and controlling—can't learn to navigate authority elsewhere in their lives.

If this all sounds impossible, I can suggest one way to see how you're doing: *Ask your teen.* Have a conversation, ask them how they're feeling about a house rule, or their thoughts on a disagreement you had a few weeks ago about something.

Think about shifting your way of communicating, so your expectations are met without you coming across as an authoritarian or dictator. *Because I said so* could shift to, *I'm asking you to be quieter for an hour because we're both sharing a workspace and I have a business call to get on.* This kind of context leads to a mutually beneficial arrangement that works for everyone.

Communicating is a big piece of the adult-teen relationship puzzle. How to communicate more effectively with your teen is coming up in Chapter 9.

A word on trying to be a "cool" parent

Well, four words: ***Don't be THAT parent!*** Your intentions might be the best, you might want to be your kid's friend to facilitate good and open conversation or hope they'll reveal more of what's happening in their lives. But this is not the style of parenting you want to go with.

Barbara Greenberg writing for *Fourways Review*[22] has some great reasons why you don't want to be the "cool" parent:

Your teen doesn't want you to be cool. They want you to act like parents, not friends. It's their turn to be a teen now, not yours. Do you really want to repeat those adolescent years? I sure don't.

Your "coolness" is embarrassing to your teen. You shouldn't be wearing clothing made for teens simply because it still fits you. Teens get embarrassed when you engage in copycat behavior.

Being cool won't open communication channels. No evidence suggests that teens confide in "cool" parents more frequently or honestly. There is more reason to believe teens confide in parents who present calm, collected, "parent-y" authority that the teen can count on.

Being cool forfeits your role as an authority figure. Teens not only need authority figures in their lives, but they thrive when parents set limits, boundaries, and a firm structure. "Cool" parents are afraid to set limits because they don't want their kids to get angry or dislike them, which does a great disservice to their teen's development.

Embrace your role as a parent. The more I'm working with teens, the more I appreciate what an amazing phase of life they're in, and how incredible their minds and hearts are. You've been given a wonderful and precious gift to be a parent. Embrace every moment, because your teen will be flying away before you know it. You get to be the one who helps them soar!

---

[22] https://fourwaysreview.co.za/368244/stop-trying-to-be-the-cool-parent-heres-why/

How to improve your relationship with your teen:

1. If you push their buttons, you push them away. Whether they say so or not, your teen looks to you for love, support, and approval. When you criticize them, pressure them to perform, or try to control them, you accomplish the opposite and none of your expectations are met. So it's a lose-lose situation. Your words have power and you can either build up a teen's confidence and self-love, or you can tear it down.

2. Work on trusting, understanding, and respecting your teen and they'll return in kind. Teens want to be seen, heard, and understood. They have to earn it, and you can share with them how, but don't expect it automatically or on your terms only. Remember they aren't children anymore and will be expected to be adults soon. Leading with trust, understanding and respect is the best way for them to learn these qualities for themselves.

3. Don't try to be the "cool" parent. Don't try to be a dictator, either! BE YOURSELF. Your teen has lived with you all their lives, so you can't hide yourself from them anyway. Your job is to be a fair, reasonable authority figure who keeps them safe and on track with their goals. Your actions model what an adult looks like.

CHAPTER 8

Relationships—Gotta Have 'Em, How to Love 'Em

While the focus of the last chapter was on you, the parent, this chapter is about relationships in general and the parent-teen relationship in particular.

Parents and teens are like peanut butter and jelly

Here is what I tell my teens:

"High school can be exciting, fun and a time when parents tend to take a back seat to your friends. It's not intentional, just a natural process of becoming young adults. However, it's important not to neglect the relationships with your parents or guardian.

"Sure, you can have amazing relationships with your friends. You can be making straight A's. You can be crushing it in sports. No matter how much success you experience, your level of overall happiness will be limited if you neglect the relationship with your parents. It's like peanut butter without jelly..."

I explain more in this teen group coaching call:

Teen Talk

Dr. RJ: You get home for school and all you want is your favorite snack. You grab two slices of bread. You pull out the peanut butter and spread it thick on one slice. You reach for the jelly, but it's not there.

Mom! you scream, where's the jelly?

She says, *we're out, honey.*

So do you eat a peanut butter sandwich, or do you save it until you find jelly?

I'm going to tell you now why I believe your parents are the jelly to your peanut butter. Ready? The relationship between teens and parents is one of the most difficult relationships you may experience. Why is that? It's because parents will always see you as a child. After all, they've known you since before you were born, they changed your diapers, fed you, and put band aids on your booboos.

But you see yourself as an adult. This leads to a relationship full of eye rolls, screaming competitions, and slammed doors. Tell me you've never done any of those things?

[Teens respond in online chat space]

Uh-huh! Now, how can you improve your relationship with your parents? A great life is a snack with BOTH peanut butter and jelly!

Don't forget to include the jelly and build a relationship with your parents too.

How to improve the relationship with your parents

There's nothing more rewarding in my work than to see teens and parents shift from a strained, contentious relationship to an open, healthy, happier relationship! Nine times out of ten, the teen wants a better relationship as much as their parents do. I advise the teen it's a two-way street—they have to do their part, and THEY can be the ones to get the ball rolling through good choices.

The following is what I teach my teens about improving their relationship with their parents as well as other adults in their life.

Take their advice. Your parents are the perfect resource. They've known you since you were an infant and whether you admit it or not, you're a lot like them. So they are the best resource you have to make good decisions. Your parents can help you brainstorm ideas, discover other resources, and create action plans. They can also help you avoid mistakes that could delay your success.

Be honest. Honesty is one of the most important gems in any relationship. I'm talking about honesty regarding your feelings. If you don't like something your parents said, then share the information with them. Most likely, they didn't mean to hurt your feelings. Try not to keep the information to yourself because it will only create resentment. Let your parents know whether you felt their decision was fair. Your parents are doing the best they can, but they cannot read your mind. The more you share with them, the more they can understand you and the person you're becoming.

Spend quality time with them. The easiest way to improve any relationship is to spend time together. Leave your phone in another room and give your parents your undivided attention. Don't be afraid to call them out if they are not giving you their attention as well!

You'll discover your parents are kind of cool and they can be fun! Get to know them, learn one of their hobbies and teach them one of yours. Share some favorite music or movies with each other. The more time you spend together, the more the relationship will grow.

A peanut butter sandwich will never taste as good as a peanut butter and jelly sandwich. Do not settle! Always add lots of delicious jelly!

"What's that interpretation?"

We don't have to go much further than our personal relationships to see how misunderstandings can happen. Teens come to me with questions and issues about their relationships with parents, teachers, and their friends. While there can be some deep, layered, difficult and harmful issues that need to be uncovered, *sometimes poor communication is the main cause of arguments and fights.*

What's going on here?

I work with teens on a concept we've talked about earlier: There isn't only ONE way, The world isn't simple, black-and-white, and all about the teen. There are many ways people think, feel, and act, and what's true for one person might differ from what's true for another.

I call this "interpretation," and to explore this idea and test it on our P-lenses, we play a game called "What's That Interpretation?"

The importance of this game is to impress upon teens how their lives and happiness are impacted by relationships with friends, parents, siblings, classmates, teachers, and coaches. If teens feel offended, angry, upset, or hurt by something someone has said or done, they have a choice in how they respond to the situation. They can explore and change how they interpret other people's words and actions in a healthy way.

Playing the game

In order to be offended by someone, you have to interpret their words and actions as offensive. I remind the teen that feeling upset or offended are simply emotions that have been triggered by an event, and they have a choice in how they respond.

Instructions: Think of a time when someone said something that made you upset, annoyed, mad, offended, or uneasy. Create a mental list of all the possibilities that led them to do what they did "to you."

Now, since you can't read the mind of that person who offended you, your interpretation of what they said or did is only a guess, an assumption. Could there be other reasons for their behavior?

Example: You're upset that your parents won't allow you to join your favorite chat app. Your initial interpretation might be to assume that your parents are trying to ruin your fun. What are other possible interpretations?

1. Your parents want to protect you from cyberbullying and online predators.

2. Your parents don't understand today's chat apps, but possibly will understand them more in the future.

3. Your parents are afraid that adding another social media account will take time away from your homework.

Choosing any of the three above interpretations would lessen the upset with your parents. You might teach them how the chat app works. Or you propose a trial period where you only use the app with them. Once they start to understand the technology, the chances of your parents saying *yes* increase.

That's how the game "What's That Interpretation?" works. You choose the interpretation AND you choose how you respond to that interpretation.

So the next time you are upset with someone, play this game.

1. List out all the possible ways to interpret the situation.

2. Choose the ones that feel most "true."

3. Decide how you want to respond—*always* in a healthy way that makes you feel good afterward.

Bonus to the teen: They begin to notice that the more they give their friends and family the benefit of the doubt, the better their relationships will be. They spend less time being angry, hurt, upset, annoyed, or offended because they have a new way of interpreting encounters with other people.

What to do when people push your buttons

This is an important lesson for teens because, they're developing healthy adult relationships. A quick online search shows the emotional button-pushing phenomenon is a persistent adult issue! Maybe we're pioneering a movement by teaching our teenagers how to do better.

Because there are so many ways to interpret any interaction in a relationship—work colleagues, family members, friends—it's helpful to think about what triggers those feelings and emotions that make us say or do things we later regret.

How do you remove all buttons in a relationship? ***By having a conversation about the buttons.***

I'm giving the responsibility to you, the parent, the adult in the room who can model how to solve this issue in a healthy, effective way. Through your example, your teen will learn how to communicate these things for themselves.

Buttons are more about you than the person pressing it. Your teen may not get this at first, but the process will help everyone realize what's really at play here.

Step 1 - Set aside time to talk with your teen. A real, sit-down conversation, not just in passing. (Note: If you and your teen are not talking at all, then this is probably not an exercise to start off with. When I'm coaching parents and teens in a contentious relationship, I usually don't lead with this technique.)

Step 2 - Ask them to identify the buttons they feel you're pushing. They may need an explanation of what "pushing buttons" means. It's essentially things you do as a parent that really ticks them off. I'm sure they'll have a list. Choose just one to work on.

Step 3 - Ask them this question about the button you've chosen: *How are you interpreting this button?* Not what you said or did, but how the teen interprets it. Gently keep them on track. If they respond, *well, YOU do this* *and YOU do that,* ask for a rephrased answer using "I": *I feel this way when you do that,* or *I think I'm not being heard or respected.*

Step 4 - Ask: *What's another possible interpretation?* The teen will need to think on it a bit, and try not to "fill in the blanks" for them. Take the lead from their ideas, and have a conversation about other ways to interpret what's behind the button.

Step 5 - Ask: *Next time, how will you respond to the interpretations you discovered?* As the teen thinks about other possible interpretations, things can change pretty quickly. Your teen may discover the reasonable interpretations of what they thought was such a big button, and let go of it right then and there.

However, the change won't happen overnight. It will take some time to connect the button with their new way of viewing it and new choices to respond.

If the answer to Step 5 doesn't happen in this conversation (not unusual), at least you'll have taken the time and the care to talk about it. Your awareness will be greater, and your relationship will be closer. Be grateful for the connection you've made and your teen will probably come back to you with more answers, or process removing the button themselves. Either way is great!

Here's an example from "Alethea," who had just gotten her driver's license:

Teen Talk

Alethea: I hate that I have to check in all the time. When I leave school, go to a friend's house, or if I'm gone longer than an hour, I have to check in when I'm on my way home. If my parents aren't home, I have to let them know that I'm home. It's literally driving me insane!

Dr. RJ: Alethea, how are you interpreting what your parents are doing?

Alethea: Well, it makes me feel like they don't trust me. Obviously if they trusted me, they wouldn't need me to check in as much, right?

We explored other interpretations of her parents' actions, and Alethea saw her parents were concerned about her safety, being a new driver. Instead of thinking, my parents don't trust me, and it makes me so mad, so frustrated, she thought, my parents are concerned about my safety because they're loving parents. It's actually very normal.

Dr. RJ: So how will you choose to respond next time?

Alethea: That it's not about trust, it's about love. I always have my phone and it actually doesn't take that long to text them.

We agreed it wasn't the act of texting, it was the interpretation of what they were asking of her. She no longer has that button.

Tips to hearing the word YES from your parents

What is the one word that teenagers are tired of hearing from their parents? "NO."

I ask my teens, what if there were a way to hack into your parents' system of "No" and crack the code to the "Yes?" Imagine if you could hear the word "yes" when asking for permission to hang out with your friends or "yes" to more time playing video games or staying up late. Would you want to hear about it?

Of course, I get a big round of "YES!" So, I tell them if they want to hear "yes" instead of "no," these are situations they will want to think about:

Issue of safety. If there is any concern that they could get hurt then they WILL hear the word "no" from you. I tell them that it's your Number One job to keep them safe.

Solution: Ask you to learn about and watch what they are doing. If they want to convince you to let them ride their skateboard with their daredevil friends, then they must first prove to you that they will be safe. So, they could invite you to join them. You could ride your bike, walk along beside them, or video your teen and their friends while they skate. Even if you do this just once, you'll get a better understanding of what they're doing, so that you feel confident they're going to be safe. You might have some great tips to give them on skateboarding more safely.

Issue of extra-curricular activities. If your teen is failing tests or not turning in their homework, then you understandably would say "no" to extra-curricular activities.

Solution: Do well in school! You don't want anything or anyone to interfere with your teen's performance in school. I tell them that the fact is, school is the focal point of their life at this moment. If they're barely passing classes, then parents are guaranteed to say "no" until they see grades improve. No way around it: The best way to improve their grades is for them to spend more time studying—make better grades and yeses will come! I encourage them to ask for help if they need it, and that you are there to support them.

Issue of obedience. If you tell your teen what to do and they don't do it, then you will say "no" to something they want to do. These are the consequences of not obeying the rules or agreements in your household.

Solution: Listen to your parents! My advice to them is clear. If you ask your teen to clean their room or do the dishes and they don't do it, then they shouldn't be surprised when they ask for something and you say "no." I advise teens to just listen and do what their parents ask. It can't get any easier than that. The benefit for them is this: If they get in the habit of being obedient, then you're likely to get into the habit of saying "yes."

Issue of trust. If they have been caught telling a big lie, then they need to expect to hear "no" for a while.

Solution: Be honest. I tell teens it's just that simple—and a very important life lesson. If they are honest then you will trust them. If you trust them, then you will be much more likely to say "yes." I share the example that if they're honest about the chat apps they're on or using their phone during the times they're allowed to, then it's easier for you to say "yes" about joining a new app, or doing something else they want to do. They also want to be honest about admitting their mistakes. You know that your teen is going to make mistakes, but if they lie about them, then they've lost your trust.

A fact about honesty and trust

I love supporting teens to be creative, self-directed, and free in their way of thinking. BUT discussing core values of honesty and trust with your teenagers is an unequivocal must. Whatever way you want to convey your personal message about honesty and trust, please have that conversation with the teen in your life.

Parents often hit a wall when they *assume* what's important to them is automatically going to be important to their teen. What inevitably follows is a continual power struggle, which doesn't help either the parent or the teen.

So I encourage you to have a discussion about honesty and trust, as well as any other values that are "unequivocal" to you. I've found teens are actually open to these realities about parent-teen relationships. They truly do want a good relationship with their parents.

Bottom line, **honesty and trust are BIG qualities that someone doesn't just hand out—they have to be earned.** When a person lies or does something untrustworthy, it takes time to build up trust and respect again.

Your teen needs to hear which values are important to you, which behaviors cross a line or break house rules, and what they need to do to hear *YES* from you.

How to improve the relationship between you and your teen

Help make a delicious peanut butter and jelly sandwich. Relationships are a two-way street. If you want your teen to take your advice, first ask if they actually want advice, or if they just want to be heard or solve the issue themselves. Brainstorming ideas *together* can be fun and rewarding. Respect your teen's feelings when they share from an honest place and be honest in return. When and if your teen plans to spend time with you, give them your undivided attention. Whether or not they admit it, your time is gold to them!

Help your teen play the game of "What's That Interpretation?" "Game" is the operative word here. Rather than "dictating" to the child, explore these ideas together. Make sure to listen and let them explore other interpretations. There is lots for both of you to learn.

Have open conversations about button-pushing. This can be challenging because of the emotions that can get riled up (this is where a professional teen coach can be helpful as an impartial expert). Use the structure I've outlined to keep the conversation within boundaries. When you take turns with the process, there's a greater chance of understanding the other's point of view (P-lens) which brings better results!

Support your teen in doing things that will get a *YES* from you. This means being fair, reasonable, and flexible. Keep them safe without being over-protective. Help them do well in school without dictating to them. Keep an open line of communication where honesty flows. Create an agreed-upon schedule of chores and responsibilities at home.

CHAPTER 9

Communication is Key

With all the new cognitive and emotional skills and new life adventures the teenager is having, communication is the tool which connects all the dots. Every moment of every day, they are expressing themselves. They are creating new relationships and making new connections that will move them out of adolescence into a healthy, happy adulthood.

Your teen is communicating with their siblings, teachers, friends, coaches, guidance counselors, the clerk in a store, the little kid next door, the bus driver, their future boss in a part-time job, the admissions officer, their first love—the list goes on and on. Not only communicating verbally, but in writing: essays, applications, texting, social media, etc.

We often take this communication thing for granted. Good *communication is another skill we aren't born with*, and teens could use some help in learning it.

You might be asking: *Are there communication skills I should be teaching my teen?*

Yes! I've pulled together some of my ideas and those of teen and communications experts, including Dale Carnegie's classic *"How to Win Friends and Influence People."*[23] Here are my ***Top Seven Communication Skills Teens Should Know and Practice***:

1. Be respectful with your words. "Rarely does it work to just say everything that is on your mind," says personal growth specialist Miranda Lamb.[24] I refer again to the Thought Triangle: Your thoughts and emotions lead to actions that can bring positive or negative results. You can teach your teen to use their words wisely, because words have the power to build up or destroy. This is a good time to be clear about

[23] https://www.amazon.com/dp/B08JLM24Q8
[24] https://thereluctantcowgirl.com/communication-skills-for-teenagers/

your expectations, setting the standard for what you believe is respectful communication and what is not.

For example, I do not like or accept "shut up" in my household. To me, it isn't positive, respectful or hold any value at all. I'm raising my kids not to use that phrase.

2. Be clear and direct. We've talked about interpretations and perceptions and how assumptions can lead to misunderstanding. No one can read minds, so it's healthy to say what you think, feel, and need. Learning to do this with intention and care—not just spewing out whatever comes to mind, but taking time to state something clearly, is valuable whether speaking, answering in class, talking on the phone, texting, or writing.

3. Ask questions. Encourage your teen not to make assumptions, but ask if they don't understand something. Asking questions is the mark of a confident person because they're not afraid of being vulnerable or "imperfect."

4. Teach your teen to use "I" statements. Remember the "pushing buttons" exercise? So many people put the blame on the other person: *YOU make me mad. YOU don't know how it feels. YOU took away my phone because you don't love me. THEY wouldn't let me join the cheerleading team. SHE hates me, so she gave me a bad grade.* Teens need to learn to be responsible for their own feelings, choices, and actions. Help them practice saying, *I feel mad when you...* or, *I'm upset that I didn't make the squad.*

5. Learn how to listen or watch for feelings. As teens move from egocentric childhood to adolescence, they become aware of their connection with others and with the world. It's a good practice for them to be mindful of the feelings of whom they're talking to—including you. If teens see the person withdraw or look hurt, the teen can make a choice: Stop or switch what they're saying, ask the person if they're okay, or acknowledge what they're noticing. Allowing another person to feel heard and understood is powerful.

6. Be willing to admit you are wrong and apologize. We all make mistakes. We all say things we don't mean or weren't clear about. Saying you're sorry—and meaning it—is the mark of a confident, caring person. By the way, this is something that parents can model for their children. I know, it can be tough to do, but I'm sure you're up for it!

7. Remember and use a person's name. Doesn't it feel great when someone remembers your name? Or when they use your name while making a point? It just feels good. Encourage your teen to learn the names of their teachers, coaches and instructors (I'm not kidding—I notice teens go through a whole school year without knowing a teacher's name!). *Thanks, Dr. Jackson, for taking the time to talk to me about this job,* really makes an adult take notice!

Tips for talking with your teen

Remember the statistic I cited earlier: In a study, 95% of teens reported feeling inferior at some point in their lives. Children are impressionable, and you don't want to be the cause of your teen's feelings of inferiority.

As a parent, your words and actions affect your teen's developing self-esteem more than anything else!

How you communicate plays a huge role. Take great care in what you do and say to your children. In this crucial developmental stage, teens are gauging their abilities and their emotional and mental fortitude.

Seven phrases your teenager should regularly hear from you

1. "I'm here for you." Teenagers are looking for independence and the freedom to make their own choices. Parents often feel their children are growing more distant and want less to do with them.

Give your teen the space to make as many of their own decisions as possible. Of course, you need to let them deal with the fallout of their decisions, and it's important to let them know you'll always be there to lend support.

2. "Will you forgive me?" When tensions are high and arguments get heated, asking your child for forgiveness can start the healing process. Setting aside your ego, or your need to be right, models the behavior for your teen.

3. "I love you." Teenagers require stability and need to know your love is unconditional. Some parents feel awkward expressing love to their teens, especially when they are nearing adulthood. However, your feelings mustn't be implied, and the best way to get comfortable expressing them is to do it regularly.

4. "Give it a go!" When teens are hesitant to take on a challenge that will teach them valuable skills, get behind them with vocal encouragement. Your role as a parent is not to shelter your kids from difficult tasks. Rather it's to show them adult life is full of challenges and the only way to overcome them is to face them head-on. The more practice they get now, the more confidence they'll have, the more successes they'll celebrate, and the better their future will be!

5. "I believe in you." This phrase is beautiful because it means no matter what, you care, you have confidence in them, you trust them, they are significant, they are enough, and they matter. Let your teen know you are their staunchest supporter, you have their back, and the most important thing is to try.

6. "I'd like to know more about how you did that." There are things your teen knows and understands better than you do. I know it's a big realization for a parent and sometimes a bit of a blow to the ego! Pretending you always know more than your teen will eventually force them to stop communicating. Whether it's social media, computers, art, mathematics, playing a musical instrument, or excellence in a sport, you can learn something new from your teen by asking them about it.

7. "I'm proud of you." Teens need to hear you're proud of them regularly, not just when they do something memorable or gain recognition for an achievement. There's a big difference between being proud when they do something special and being proud of who they are. Positive behaviors like generosity, kindness, and courage are achievements of a very special kind, and should be recognized at every opportunity with an "I'm proud of you."

Top tips for talking with your teen more effectively

Ask questions. This follows #6 above. Your teen wants so much to be seen and heard by you, in ways that don't criticize, judge, put pressure on them, or disrespect their perspective and ideas. Asking questions out of curiosity is a great way to approach a subject. It compliments them, allows them to express their ideas and praise themselves. BONUS: You get to know them better and learn from what they have to say!

Listen with attention, silence, and patience. Paying attention is an intentional exercise. It means you deliberately set down your phone or the spoon, or even park the car at the side of the road to fully turn your attention on the important thing your teen wants to say. Because you know your child so well and you know more about life than they do, it's tempting to jump in with a "solution." Try to be patient and hear them out. You might even be surprised at something they bring up, which will change your response.

Pause, and stay calm. A moment of patience during an angry exchange saves a thousand moments of regret. We've talked about button-pushing, and I know your teen can push yours with just a word or a roll of the eyes! Take control of the situation before it goes sour. Just stop, pause, and stay calm. You have the choice to stop the conversation if you need to. Be honest with your teen and say, *I need to postpone this for a little while so I can cool down* (or *change my mood* or *think about this some more,* or whatever you need to do to remove yourself from the situation). The key here is not to forget about it and leave things hanging. Make sure you go back and complete the conversation at a time you both agree on.

Do you play the Circle Game in your relationships?

This is a question I ask my teens, and I also ask parents, mentors, and myself. *If so, STOP!*

We get the biggest satisfaction but also the biggest aggravation from relationships. Whether with friends, parents, children or siblings, relationships have one of the biggest impacts on daily happiness. When our relationships are healthy and fun, we are happy. When they are contentious, we are unhappy. It's just that simple.

Teens are just developing the skills and discernment to foster healthy relationships. They are learning how to communicate responsibly while coping with hormones, moods, and new feelings. This is the reason I teach teens about the "Circle Game."

The Circle Game: Fight or Flight vs Stay and Communicate

I invite you to be a fly on the wall while I describe the "Circle Game" to teenagers:

Teen Talk

Dr. RJ: I'm going to tell you about a "real life" game people play that can be the biggest waste of time in any relationship. It's a game we ALL play without even knowing we're playing it, and a game nobody can win.

There are three basic stages of the "Circle Game." Say that you and I are best friends, and today I saw you laughing with the one person I dislike the most. Of course, you know I dislike them, and it hurts my feelings to see you having a good time together.

Stage 1: Act Like I Don't Care. You ask what's wrong. I say nothing—even though it's clearly something.

I want you to know that I'm mad without me having to say so. I want YOU to notice something is off. I can't be too obvious about being mad because then you'll jump to Stage 3 and the game is over. For example, we usually have a silly greeting, but now I just coolly say hi instead. Now you know something is off.

Stage 2: Create Some Distance. I passively initiate some psychological rejection toward you so you can share my hurt feelings. You then ask why I'm doing this to you.

Let's say we normally skateboard together after school. Now, I text you and say I'm just going to chill at home.

You ask: Are you SURE you're okay? You've been acting weird.

I put my surprised face on. Huh? Me? Nah I'm good. Why do you ask?

You start to realize you may have messed up. I say to myself, YES!

Stage 3: Wait for Friend to Feel as Crummy as I Do. The goal is to get you to confront me—even though I'm the one with the problem. If I "give in" and initiate the conversation, I'll lose the game! You must start the confrontation. To get you to do this, I make it obvious I'm mad and continue to create distance by ignoring your texts. Then the next day, I see you at school and act like nothing happened. Finally, you've had it and initiate the confrontation: Hey, Dr RJ, what's up with you? What's really going on?

That's when I "win!"

You insist we talk, then I come clean and finally tell you how betrayed I felt when you were talking to an enemy of mine. You apologize. I apologize. Then we're back to being friends.

Hmmm… Seems like we could've saved a lot of time and upset feelings if I told you the truth in the first place.

Why do we play these silly games?

Does this sound familiar? Have you ever seen your teen do this or be on the receiving end of it?

You helplessly watch the two friends circle each other, playing "hurt ego," each passive-aggressively forcing the other to confront them, and you even witness the friendship end as a result.

Teens waste hours, days, even weeks playing the Circle Game! It's easier to skip the game and just tell their friend how they are feeling, so why is it so difficult to do?

As with so many of the issues around honest, open communication, the ego pops up with intentions of protecting us from feeling hurt, rejected, weak, vulnerable, or unsafe. The ego gets bored (interestingly, the healthier we become the more the ego needs a job to do!) and perceives threat in the merest upsetting action or word. The ego makes it difficult for teens to tell friends how they feel, So the teen goes on the defensive, wastes time and possibly sacrifices a good friendship.

Here is where the Thought Triangle comes in handy again. When teens recognize their ego is causing them to run or fight, they can get back in control their thoughts, emotions, actions and, of course, the results.

They get to choose to stay and communicate responsibly, thus, stopping the game before it even starts.

We want them to know their feelings are normal and it's perfectly understandable to be hurt by words or actions. Everyone experiences sadness, disappointment, anger, embarrassment. It's okay to feel hurt, but there is no need for their ego to take over.

This is especially true for our loved ones: Deep down, they love us and never want to see us truly hurt. This is the time to use tools and skills such as our P-lens and exploring what interpretation we're choosing to make of the situation.

How to skip the Circle Game

My simple advice is this: The best way to improve relationships is never to let your ego take control. Instead, stay in control and talk.

The more we communicate our thoughts and feelings the less conflict we'll have, and the happier our relationships will be.

It takes practice— egos are persistent! We may need to remind ourselves that our friends and family are not threats and like us, they sometimes allow their egos to take control and do and say hurtful things. We're human, we all do it! Nonetheless, we know our loved ones' heartfelt intentions are not to see us in pain.

So the next time a family member offends or disappoints you with their words or actions (or lack thereof), remind yourself they are not a threat. Your ego doesn't have to take over and the situation doesn't have to be fight-or-flight. Instead, *stay and communicate* so your relationships will continue to thrive.

How to support your teen in communicating effectively

Help them practice communication skills. Communication is another skill no one is born with, and one that teens need to learn for a successful, happy future. Help them understand that their words have power and create results, whether they intended the result or not. If they are respectful with their words, communicate clearly and directly, take responsibility for their ideas, ask questions to get clarity, and mindful of responses received, they have a great chance of getting the results they want!

Talk to your teen with intention. Remember as a parent, your words and actions affect your teen's developing self-esteem more than anything else! Intentional communication starts with being mindful of your teen's fragile emotions and ego, (not to mention their hormones!). Communicate in a way that lifts them up and helps them learn while feeling good about themselves. When you model management of your emotions and ego, they'll learn how it's done! Your relationship with your teen will improve as well.

Remember the seven phrases and top three tips for talking with your teen more effectively. 1) Ask questions out of curiosity; 2) listen with attention, silence, and patience; 3) pause and stay calm in moments of high-level emotions. By the way, you don't have to engage every time your teen wants to have a conversation. It's okay to set boundaries for yourself and choose when conversations happen so you can be fully present. Respect your teen by keeping the commitment to the scheduled conversation.

Avoid the Circle Game. Our egos can get in the way of being honest about our feelings—we're human, we all do it in some form or another! Now that you know about the Circle Game, you can see when your teen is going down that path and help them **stay and communicate.**

Goals, Success, and Happiness

CHAPTER 10

Goals and Motivation

Working with thousands of teenagers, I can honestly say they rarely have real goals. Plans for the evening or where they want to go on vacation—these are wants, hopes, wishes and whims. When I say *goals,* I mean things teens really want to attain, things that light a fire in their belly and motivate them to do what it takes to achieve them. Something exciting that's worth pursuing.

Teens have wants, desires, hopes, and dreams, but they don't know what to do with them.

It's not their fault. Not so long ago, they were children whose thinking was "oriented to the here and now—that is, to things and events that they can observe directly."[25] Now they are better able to think about what's possible, to consider the future hypothetically and critically. They're learning how to plan ahead, juggling different variables to create an outcome. They understand cause and effect, and the consequences of their actions.

They are learning to think for themselves about the future.

But just like confidence, which we discussed in Chapter 1, setting and achieving goals doesn't come naturally in this developmental stage, rather they are new skills that have to be learned.

I believe a teen who's focused on problems of the past instead of possibilities of the future, one who is adrift in the day-to-day without something to look forward to that excites them, is often a teen who is susceptible to:

- Unhappiness
- Stress
- Anxiety
- Lack of self-control
- Fear and doubt

---

[25] https://psychology.jrank.org/pages/14/Adolescence.html

- Faithlessness
- Depression or other behavioral issues

We adults understand what it takes to achieve goals. Goals give you direction and a place for your mind to focus. They ignite your passion, spark excited anticipation, and create confidence in knowing where you're going. Sometimes you achieve your goals and sometimes you don't. Either way, merely focusing on the goal gets you closer to your dream because of focusing on the goal, right?

Setting clear goals increases a teen's chances of getting what they really want (not just what they believe they're *expected* to want, from school, society, or...well...parents).

When your teen shifts their focus to possibilities of the future, their mood changes, their attitude changes, their emotions change. I have seen it hundreds of times and it's amazing to witness.

The power of goals

The reason I have so much success in coaching teens is because of my ability to help them manage their thoughts. I don't prescribe a magic pill. I don't have them lie on a couch and tell me about their problems. I don't berate their parents and say it's their fault.

My secret is shifting the teen's focus away from what's holding them back from fulfilling their potential, and *toward* what they really want (which, as it turns out, WILL lead them to realizing their full potential).

We work together to turn wants, desires, hopes, and dreams into actual GOALS that have meaning. The goal might not be to become president of the United States, be the richest person in the world, or set up a colony on Mars (although none of these are impossible)—it could be something just outside their comfort zone or beyond their reach.

I know a young man who, as a teen, struggled with his parents' divorce, uninterested in going out or doing well in school. Then he decided he wanted to buy his own car. He immersed himself in achieving this goal with confidence and purpose: He got a good part-time job, saved his money, researched everything he could about cars, and actually made the purchase and accomplished the goal before he graduated from high school.

Eventually, this boy went on to engineering school and landed a job with Rolls Royce! When he first committed to the goal, no one—including him—knew his path would go this way.

I coach teens on achieving their goals, starting with these three basic steps:

1. Set intention.

2. Create an action plan.

3. Make a time frame.

1. Set intention. An intention is a destination. When teens set an intention, they are giving directions to their mind toward that destination. It's like going on a road trip. Included in their intention is WHY they want to go there, which is key to keeping up momentum.

2. Create an action plan. Keeping with the road trip analogy, this is the time to map out which highways the teen will take. Where they'll stop to eat, which detours for sightseeing and gas stops. The action plan is step-by-step instruction to get to their destination.

3. Make a time frame. This is simply how long it will take to reach their destination. A time frame puts parameters around the action plan and keeps the teen on track. Time frames and deadlines sometimes need to be flexible: The teen who wanted to buy his own car had set an original deadline for when he got his driver's license. He soon realized this wasn't reasonable, so he set a new deadline of graduation—and achieved his goal ahead of time.

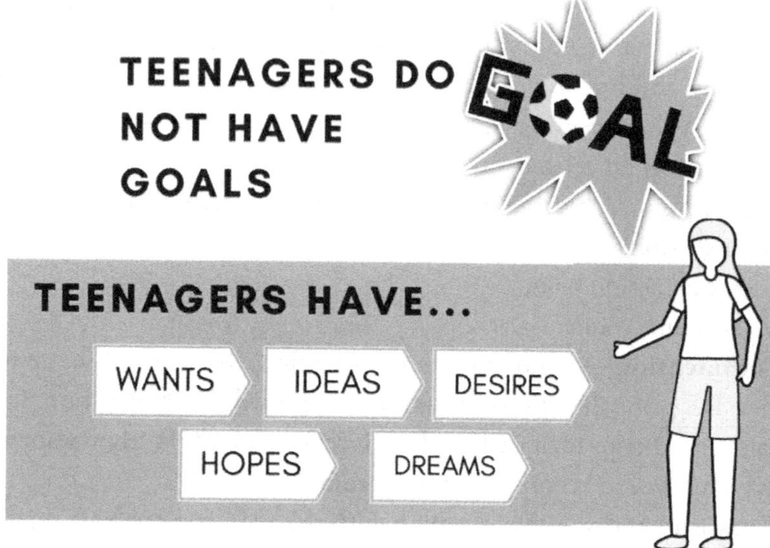

BUT NOT GOALS

Coaching helps turn their wants, desires, hopes, and dreams into GOALS

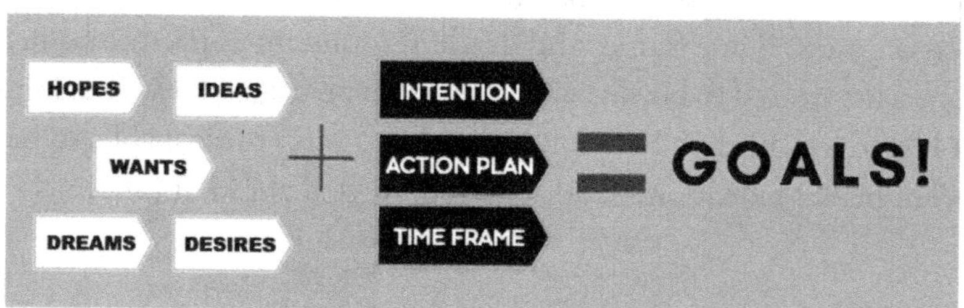

GOALS have three components:

When teenagers have GOALS it increases their chances of getting what they want, desire, hope and dream

Motivation and Meaning

Parents and teenagers live in very different worlds, and parents naturally set expectations and goals for their children from their own P-lens. It seems obvious their teen should want the same things and be motivated to achieve those goals.

Here's the disconnect: Parents are setting these goals, perceptions, and expectations from their many years of adult experience. They've learned the hard way through their own mistakes and setbacks. They've lived in the real world long enough to know its "rules."

Let's add another factor: This is your *baby* we're talking about here! The precious soul you raised, nurtured, and sacrificed for. *Who knows what's best for your teen than you, right?*

While that may be so, the teen doesn't have the same life experience or motivation as you. It's up to you to educate, teach, and *negotiate* with your teen along the way.

Negotiating doesn't mean pushing, bribing, or setting ultimatums. It means **meeting the teen where they are.**

Before I can really get into helping teens set and achieve goals, I have to help them understand motivation, especially how you sometimes have to do stuff you don't want, in order to get what you ultimately want.

In this group teen coaching session, we talk about staying motivated with things they won't want to do, which, no surprise, are usually requests coming from their parents:

Teen Talk

Dr. RJ: A lot of parents tell me they get tired of telling their teens the same things over and over. They don't want to micromanage you! What does that mean, micromanage?

In my practice I have people who work for me and each has their own talents and their own job to do. I trust them to do it. I don't watch every little thing they do, and remind them over and over what they know needs to be done. That's micromanaging.

Let me ask: Would you like to be micromanaged?

[Teens respond in online chat space]

Right, I didn't think so! And guess what? Your parents don't want to micromanage you either.

So, what do we do about this? I know you know what you're supposed to be doing. I also know that you avoid doing the things your parents constantly nag you to do because they're just not fun. Am I right? They're either painful or you see no value in them.

What are things you aren't motivated to do?

Okay, we have chores, putting away the dishes, mopping, taking out the garbage, math homework, cleaning my room, walking the dog, feeding the dog, taking tests, brushing my teeth (that one hurt as an orthodontist!).

Teens have to WANT the motivation. The task has to mean something to them. This is the stage of their life when they're learning to think more critically, to plan ahead, and to understand cause and effect. Context and meaning are really important here.

I share my own story: I used to really dislike washing dishes. I knew how to do it, but I didn't enjoy it at all. When I was single, I'd use plastic dishes, but that no longer worked when I got married because my wife is super pro-environment—no plastic, no Styrofoam.

Of course, a growing family would mean LOTS more dishes, so I had to make a change. I saw three options: 1) fight it; 2) do it but be mad all the time; 3) learn to like it. I chose to do it and learn to like it. This is part of being in a relationship, taking responsibility, and maturing as an adult.

Teens are in a relationship with the household, and when it comes to things they don't like to do, they have the same three options:

They can fight their parents, which they quickly take off the table because they don't want the consequences.

They can do those things in a mad, grumpy, complaining mode, making themselves miserable.

They can try my secret: ***intrinsic motivation.***

Intrinsic motivation

In psychology, intrinsic motivation is known as the best type of motivation. "Intrinsic" means inherent by nature, something that comes from within. According to *Parenting for Brain*[26], "intrinsic motivation is an inner drive that propels a person to pursue an activity, not for external rewards, but because the action itself is enjoyable."

If our teens only do things because they want the approval of others, or they think they're "supposed" to do them, or they're getting paid, or they'll be externally rewarded in some other way... if these are a teen's only guiding principles or motivators, they will NEVER achieve true meaning or happiness in their adult lives.

How to develop intrinsic motivation

The secret to being motivated is conditioning your mind to reframe unpleasant tasks in a positive light.

It starts with looking at the chore or obligation and how you feel about it. For me, washing dishes was painful, horrible, until I decided it did me no good to think that way every single time I washed a dish.

Fun things make me feel good, so I chose to condition my mind to think of washing dishes as fun. Believe me, it was a lie at first! But here's what we know about human nature: *We have a natural tendency to move away from pain and toward pleasure.* If we encourage our mind to think of something as pleasurable, then our mind will begin to believe it.

I tell my teens **they have the superpower to change the way they think about unpleasant tasks.** If they frame brushing their teeth or walking the dog as something pleasurable, they will naturally move toward that feeling. I remind them their minds have been programmed in all kinds of ways since they were babies, so they DO have the power to shift their thinking.

---

[26] https://www.parentingforbrain.com/intrinsic-motivation/

It's as simple as, *I like walking the dog because I love my dog,* or, *I like running the mile in practice because I want to win the race next month.* It doesn't always work at first, but with practice, teens begin to look for ways to confirm and appreciate the tasks they face.

Back to the washing dishes example. One day I said to my wife, let's do the dishes together. We listened to music and talked while we worked. It was really great! Now the washing up is a tradition we both look forward to. When I began my shift in thinking, I definitely didn't imagine or anticipate such a rewarding outcome.

You never know what's going to happen when you become motivated to do something. You can't imagine where changing your mind will take you—this is truly the secret of motivation.

What happens when a teen who feels full of self-doubt and "not enoughness" decides to change their thinking? As I tell my teens, the answer is: The sky's the limit!

Imagine changing **I could never accomplish this** to **I'm special, I'm unique, I can do anything I set my mind to, I have what it takes.**

I love to see a teen's eyes light up when they begin to imagine themselves this way!

Research suggests it takes a minimum of 21 days[27] to shift the mind into new habits, so I suggest teens try out this motivating technique for three weeks. At first it might not work, it might feel awkward. But science supports it, so it is worth trying.

Here's another reason why the technique is worth trying: It's difficult to live doing things that have to be done and to resist, dislike, or procrastinate doing those things. Teens know they have to grow up at some point and take on more responsibilities like career, family, achieving their goals, and fulfilling their biggest dreams. I remind them that it's only taken about 13-14 years to program them into the thinking they have now—how difficult will it be when they're in their 20s or 30s? Much more difficult! The older we get, the harder it is to reprogram our thinking.

I believe intrinsic motivation is a wonderful concept for anyone to embrace.

---

[27] https://www.healthline.com/health/how-long-does-it-take-to-form-a-habit

I hope you feel the same way and will support your teen in developing and practicing the skillset, which will build a foundation for their success.

Maintaining motivation: recharging your mental batteries

Teens are busy people, juggling homework, activities, social and family life. They want to achieve their goals, but they're bound to experience phases when they're feeling unmotivated. I tell my teens this is perfectly normal.

What do you do when your phone battery is low? Easy—find an outlet or charging station and fill it back up. ***What about when your mental battery is running low? Where's the charging station for that?***

Here's how to get motivated about your goals again:

1. See it! Visualize goal achievement.

Visualization allows you to get excited about your goal again. It reminds you why you wanted to achieve the goal in the first place. Find a time when it's quiet and you're alone. You can even have some calming music in the background. Take a few deep breaths to clear your mind. Once you feel calm, think about your goal. See yourself achieving that goal. Be as detailed as possible. What are you doing? What are you wearing? Who are you with? How are you feeling? The more detailed the better!

2. Talk about it! Share your goals through conversation.

Talk about your goals to your parents, friends, classmates, teachers, coaches, and even people you don't know that well! This will definitely recharge your battery. Anytime you talk about your goals, desires, or dreams, the more real they become. If you find yourself losing motivation, just start talking about it to anyone who will listen—and who respect what you're doing (naysayers and negative people are motivation killers!). Who knows, one of these people may have something to offer in achieving that goal.

3. Do it! Take decisive action, no matter how BIG or small.

Since your goal is in the distant future, it makes sense you might lose motivation. That's why it's important to take some action right away toward making it happen. When you accomplish anything that contributes to your goal, it will recharge your battery. It can be simply doing some research, making a to-do list, or writing something down in your calendar. Accomplishing small tasks each day will not only get you motivated about your goal, but will also help you achieve it!

Don't allow a low battery to prevent you from achieving your goal. Tap into your own "charging station" any time you feel the need. These three steps will have you up and energized in no time!

The missing piece to your success in achieving goals

To keep us on track with our goals, we've talked about identifying meaningful goals, creating a roadmap to achieve them, developing intrinsic motivation and recharging low-energy batteries.

What's next? ***Connecting with the right people.***

I'm not just talking about the "usual" people—a favorite teacher, guidance counselor, spiritual mentor, coach, instructor. While these people may be crucial to achieving goals, most teens overlook or undervalue the "missing piece" of their social network: ***the people they ignore!*** These types of people are:

- Classmates they don't talk to or even don't like very much
- The stranger they ignore or are rude to
- The teacher they hope not to get next year, because they're so demanding
- The school janitor they never notice
- The nerd or the jock they have nothing in common with

Yes, these people make up the missing piece to your teen's success, for three reasons:

1. They are rarer than the rarest gem, oftentimes with better information than Google! Each is made up of a unique combination of experiences unlike our own. Too often, we surround ourselves with people who think and act like us, and basically tell us what we already know and are comfortable with. A person who puts a new P-lens onto our outlook is a gem.

2. Some personalities can bring out our best qualities. A person whom we believe is annoying or boring may actually propel us toward reaching our goal. Maybe we're quiet and shy, and our missing piece is a person who will bring out our more assertive side. Maybe we're passionate and outgoing, and our missing piece is the person who will bring out our calmer, introspective side.

3. These people also have a network of friends and family. We never know who they may know. Achieving dreams, desires, or goals often relies on who we know more than what we know. So why ignore certain people? Why be rude and dislike someone? Why not talk to all of your classmates? Go out of your way to speak to a person you feel isn't so cool. They may know someone who knows someone who will help you achieve your goal. You never know what you'll learn about your goal—or about yourself—that moves you closer to your dream.

Treat everyone as if they were your missing piece to success.

How to help your teen develop meaningful goals and achieve them successfully

1. Set realistic expectations around your teen's goals. Always remember you're their support system, not their critic. They're still trying to get used to how things are in the real world so meet them where they are. Listen to what they think they can achieve rather than what you want them to achieve.

2. Support them in setting intentions, creating an action plan, and making a time frame. These are tangible pieces of taking a wish or dream forward into a "real" goal. As the adult, you already have experience and can advise them how to go about doing this. BONUS: Because these steps aren't emotion-based, you can work on something amazing together without stirring up emotional drama.

3. Understand intrinsic motivation and its power. We have the power to be motivated to do anything when we condition our mind to frame tasks within the pleasure of meeting a goal. Help your teen practice building that foundation to get the positive, happy-making things they truly want.

4. Help them find the missing piece of success. They may not realize it, but you know how rich life can be when we don't stick to the status quo, don't stay in our silos, and ignore or disrespect people who think differently. Encouraging teens to step outside their comfort zones and limited P-lenses can be life-changing on so many amazing levels!

CHAPTER 11

What is Success?

Since "success" is a concept so loaded with connotation and interpretation, it's useful to take a moment and go back to basics. The dictionary definition of success is ***the accomplishment of an aim or purpose; the good or bad outcome of an undertaking.*** Merriam-Webster[28]adds: *also, the attainment of wealth, favor, or eminence.* Whoa, feels like we're already going down a deep rabbit hole!

My life's work with teens is founded in happiness (smiling on the inside AND outside) and fulfilling my life's purpose. Does that mean wealth, favor, or eminence? Sure, but sadly, I see teens who ONLY see the material results of their goals. A great example comes from this article, "Parents, our definition of success is all wrong[29]": "Something funny has happened over the past couple of generations—where we went from defining success as "a chicken in every pot" to a heavy, guilt-inducing load of expectations...a full slate of AP classes, more SAT tutors, Ivy League school, prestigious professional six-figure career, and a McMansion with two living rooms.

"If we or our kids deviate off this path, we ask ourselves: Where did we fail? Some parents are even getting desperate, like those celebrities who didn't think their children had enough opportunities through wealth and fame, so they allegedly bribed colleges to ensure their kids' admission...For our sanity—and that of our kids—we need to stop this relentless pressure to achieve more, and more, and more."

Powerful, right? In short, ***we may need to redefine success.*** We still want our kids to set and achieve goals, and be the best they can be. This likely requires getting A's in school, finding a good job, managing their finances, having dreams and ambitions, and all of that.

---

[28] https://www.merriam-webster.com/dictionary/success
[29] https://www.washingtonpost.com/lifestyle/2019/05/08/why-our-definition-success-is-all-wrong/

At the same time, I think it's important for teens to develop their own definition of success. What it truly looks and feels like for them.

My job—and the job of every adult who interacts with teens—is to nurture the purpose within success. Purpose, meaning, and happiness are what we strive for in life, and *must* be behind our definitions of success.

Business mentor Debbie Allen, writing for *Entrepreneur.com*[30], advises adults on success: "I can tell you one thing: Success isn't what others tell you it is. It's what you say it is for yourself! If you believe success is what everyone else says it is, you'll always miss the target. And when you do achieve someone else's version of success, it won't mean as much to you."

I definitely believe this is true for teenagers, and what better time than now to help them explore what success means to them? My own definition of success is teaching teenagers to find the meaning and purpose that comes from self-love, confidence, and happiness.

Are you with me?

Interpretations of success

Remember playing the "What's That Interpretation" game and exploring other ways teens can learn discernment? Success is another area where interpretation comes into play, big time.

As seen in the quotes above, teens get A LOT of definitions of what success should look like. The messages come from society, media, school, or well-intentioned adults in the teen's life. Some examples are extreme, some are useful, but these days teens get a lot of input about what success is *supposed* to look like, .

My goal is to unpack those messages and generalizations so teens can discern what makes sense for them. In this teen group coaching session, we are learning about interpretations of success:

---

[30] https://www.entrepreneur.com/article/340819

Teen Talk

Dr. RJ: Two weeks ago, we all agreed that we wanted to make straight A's this year. We're shooting for the moon. We all want the best this year, right?

So today we're talking about what hinders us from making straight A's. The reason isn't your teacher or because you're online. Those are excuses!

The reason you are not taking the actions necessary to make straight A's, is because you are distracted by the negativity from your interpretations.

Interpretations are similar to guessing. We talked about this when it comes to your friends. Say you text a friend and they don't respond and just leave you hanging. Before, you'd start heaping negative guesses on yourself: *Oh, they don't like me. They don't want to be my friend. I'm not important enough, not the top in the friend group.*

But now you don't do that anymore, right? Why?

[Teens respond in online chat space]

Right, because you have no clue why someone leaves you hanging. You're not in their head. It could be any number of reasons, none of which have anything to do with you. Good job!

When you get all caught up in those negative guesses about people and situations, it literally slows you down and makes you feel bad. How can you do well in school if you feel bad?

If you feel good, you're going to take action. Change your interpretations so your mind can focus on what's important and what you have control of. Don't choose interpretations that make you feel bad. Instead, choose positive ones like, *my friend is probably having a bad day. They weren't trying to be mean to me, maybe I just took it the wrong way.* Send your friend positive energy and move on with your day.

Remember, this success game is 80% mental. If you can conquer the mind, you're going to crush it in life.

Understanding how interpretation affects everyday life and controls thoughts and emotions, is the first step. We then get into it more deeply, discussing interpretation's role in achieving goals and pursuing passions—which is what happiness is all about. I tell teens ***my goal is to help them succeed in every area of their life.***

Here's another example of different interpretations of success:

"Jason" has been playing soccer since he was six. He knows he's really good at it and he believes his only chance to go to college is through a soccer scholarship. But this season he's been dreading *every single* practice and game. What's happening here?

Working together, we discover soccer isn't what Jason wants anymore. He wants to spend more time getting good grades and working to save money to travel. The goal or dream he had isn't working for him anymore, but he's afraid to let it go. Jason *interpreted* success as a soccer scholarship. He's afraid to tell his parents about his change of heart because he's "interpreted" soccer as what they want for him.

Our next step is to explore other interpretations and options that will get him feeling excited and passionate. He may realize he really does love soccer and becomes passionate about playing again. He may realize there are other means to get a scholarship. He may discover a whole other interest and start to dig into that with excitement and passion—which might lead him directly to his life's path.

Here is where the parent, guardian or mentor plays a key role. You can help your teen sort this out for themselves without feeling guilty, ashamed, or acquiescing to what they *interpret* as your version of success.

A word about leadership

I could write a book about leadership and teens. Well, in a way, I have! What are the traits of a great leader?

- Self-confidence
- Positive beliefs
- Clear perception and discernment

- Ability to understand and manage our emotions
- Effective communication
- Good relationships and community
- Passion around our vision
- Meaningful goals and action plans to achieve them
- Clear sense of what success means
- Purpose and happiness

Essentially, these all are traits of someone living up to their fullest potential, which is what we've been talking about for our beloved teenagers!

We talk about our children being the future leaders of the world. I believe our teenagers are leaders NOW. Teens influence others all day, every day—making an impact on parents, family, friends, mentors, teachers, coaches, neighbors, community, even the stranger in the coffee shop.

I believe teens are old enough to realize *they ARE leaders and influencers right now.* The realization isn't meant to *pressure* them to act a different way or take on more responsibility, rather it's meant to *empower* them to know the unique and important person they already are. Thinking of themselves as leaders is a key to stepping into powerful leadership roles in the future.

These are some key points about leadership that I frequently remind the teens I work with:

Success is something you can have in school, in sports, and with your family and friends. You can have success in your hobbies and interests and in achieving the things you truly desire.

The key to all of this success comes down to leadership.

Leadership is influence. You have influence over everyone around you, whether you know it or not. You influence your parents, your friends, your classmates, your teachers, and your coaches. Who do you influence most? YOU, because you are controlling your own thoughts, beliefs, and feelings!

The leadership mindset begins on the inside.

How you influence yourself ultimately determines how you influence others. Improving as a leader starts with improving yourself.

You are a leader, even if you do not realize it. What you say and do has a meaningful effect on people around you, and you get to choose whether the effect is positive or negative.

How to help your teen develop
a healthy relationship with success

1. Think about your own definition of "success" for your teenager. This is a big ask, I know. We've spent our lives with an imprint of what success is from our own experience and background. You may be one of those people who was influenced by your parent's concept of success—did it work for you or not? An open mind about what success means in this day and age is key to your unique teen discovering what success is for them.

2. Practice interpretation when it comes to success. Is your teen clear about what success means to them and how it influences their daily life? There's no right or wrong answer, and the exploration can be fun and enlightening for both of you (try playing the "What's That Interpretation" game from a success perspective).

3. Be ready for them to change their goals. Your teen may have had an idea of success since early childhood, or is just figuring out what it is now. What they decide may or may not meet your approval. Before you dig in your heels, ask: Does it make them happy? Do they feel passionate about it? Are they motivated, and are taking action to pursue it?

4. Let them know they ARE a leader. They need to know what they do matters. Their actions influence others. Improving themselves to be the best they can be is the way to become a successful leader and influencer!

CHAPTER 12

Harvesting Happiness

Have you ever counted how often you smile each day?

Did you know babies smile more than four hundred times a day, but adults smile fewer than twenty?[31] I guess that's not an unusual statistic coming from an orthodontist who specializes in smiles…

What it tells me is we experience true happiness as babies, but as we get older, somehow our happiness decreases. I'm interested in what happens between babyhood and adulthood that influences the desire to smile out of happiness.

We're constantly bombarded with the idea of happiness, in movies, songs, and fairy tales where the end goal is to "live happily ever after." If happiness is such a big part of life, doesn't it seem odd it isn't "taught" in school? From what I understand, people don't ask teens very often, *are you happy?* I don't think they ask each other either. Happiness is the one thing that everyone in the world wants and needs, and we don't talk about it.

I admit, happiness is a big concept to wrap our arms around, yet I believe it's the foundation of who we are, what we think, and how we create our life's purpose. It's a topic I'm eager to get into with my teens, as an integral part of their developing thoughts, beliefs, perspective, goals, definition of success, and purpose in life.

Many people believe happiness is all about getting what you want. I get it. It feels good to hear the word *yes*. It's natural to want things to go our way. But happiness is much more than getting what you want when you want it.

This is a concept many teens are just beginning to grasp, as they move from the instant gratification of childhood toward more nuanced concepts of adulthood.

I explore this idea in a teen group coaching session:

---

[31] https://www.thejournal.ie/mental-health-smile-1550017-Jul2014

Teen Talk

Dr. RJ: How many of you think happiness is getting what you want? When everything is "YES" and things always go your way? Sounds awesome. Well, let's look at that.

Imagine if you asked if you could eat cake for breakfast, cookies for lunch, candy for a snack, and ice cream for dinner, and your mom said "yes". Do you think you would feel happiness when you went to bed? No! Your stomach would cause you to feel regret for sure. Sometimes the word "no" can actually make you happy, simply because yes would have caused you pain.

Sometimes getting what you want can cause you to be unhappy later. Interesting, right?

According to my definition, ***happiness is a state of mind of receiving or creating positive thoughts.*** I want teens to know they are the creators of their own happiness—it's an inside job.

The group discussion continues:

Teen Talk

Dr. RJ: Two kids move to a new school. "Jack" is excited about the adventure and looks forward to meeting new friends. "Joe" is angry about having to leave his old school.

So did the *event* of moving to a new school cause the kids to feel a certain way? Or was it the kids' *thoughts* that caused them to feel a certain way?

[Teens respond in chat space]

Right, you're correct! Jack thinks positively about the move and experiences happiness. Joe thinks negatively about his move and experiences unhappiness.

Here's another example: Two kids don't make the varsity basketball team. "Olivia" is disappointed at first, but decides to practice harder and is excited to try out again next year. "Paige" is mad and vows never to play the sport again.

Did the *event* of not making the team cause their responses? Or did the *thoughts* about not making the team cause their responses?

As you know, thoughts are constantly going in and out of your mind. Positive thoughts release "feel good" biochemicals in the brain like dopamine and serotonin, which make you feel good, hopeful, laughing, silly, loving—you know, happy! Negative or unhappy thoughts make the brain release "stress" hormones like cortisol, which bring the opposite response. Let's choose to bring forward more positive and happy thoughts, okay?

Happiness and pursuing your goals

Because happiness is extremely important for a teen's success in pursuing goals, it's important they have a way to maintain happiness when things have them feeling less than good. ***The easiest way to maintain happiness is the simple practice of gratitude.***

When teens start having doubts about pursuing a goal, I suggest they stop and take a break. Yes, just stop.

1. Pause. Take a look at your life and notice everything that's right.

Notice the big things and the little things: having fun playing video games with your brother, the vacation you're going on in a few weeks, your cat acting adorable on the bed, your mom cooking your favorite food for dinner tonight, your history class that's going well with an awesome teacher, the awesome pair of shoes you just bought, your English class that's almost over so soon you won't have to have that teacher you don't like much.

When you start to appreciate what you already have, you're going to feel good. Gratitude will have you feeling happier, and that happiness will be the boost to keep moving forward.

Now get back on the saddle and do your next task toward your goal. Keep that gratitude up! Once you're feeling happy again, you'll notice self-doubt actually decreases.

Why does this work? Because happiness attracts more happiness—you could say it's contagious, or that it builds like a snowball in the best possible way. No matter what the goal is, when you peel back the layers and ask yourself, *why do I want this,* the answer is happiness. Teens love hearing they have permission to pursue happiness.

Happiness is available even when the going gets tough

Have you ever been told you should enjoy the process of pursuing your goal, but you find the process is rarely fun? This is true for most of us at some point or another. We wish everything would move along smoothly but we know that life isn't actually like that. Everything has its seasons and cycles and ups and down. It's almost impossible to maintain the same pattern or routine or emotional state—we're not even wired for that!

But as we've discussed, teens are new to this world of emotions, adult feelings, moods, plans and goals. In this coaching session, I share a way to look at the bumps in the road toward success:

Teen Talk

Dr. RJ: We're going to talk about motorcycles, because you know I love motorcycles! I want you to think about the RPM on a motorcycle—the measure of how fast the bike is going. When you look at the gauge, you see that some of the numbers are in red. Anyone know what that means?

[Teens respond in online chat space]

Right—good job! The red numbers are the engine's maximum speed.

Can you ride in the red? Of course you can, but it's not advisable for long periods of time. You've got to ride in the green zone too.

Your mind and body are like the motorcycle. When you're pursuing a goal, there's a green zone RPM that's always comfortable to ride in. When you first decide to pursue a goal, you get excited and begin to brainstorm ideas. Then you do the research to create an action plan.

You start to tell your friends and family about your goal, and everyone is happy for you.

You're feeling the wind and enjoying the ride. It's all going smoothly and you're imagining how better life will be, so you go a little faster, loving the momentum, and you get near the red zone. Wow, you notice a change. There are more potholes to dodge, more obstacles, and more detours. Something might even be wrong with your bike and it's going to cost money to get it fixed, money you may not have!

Doubt and fear begin to consume your mind. You begin to question if you can even achieve the goal. You start asking yourself if this is even worth your time, and you begin making excuses on why you should give up. Your goal seems to be moving further and further away. You're discouraged and become unhappy as you see that "better life" disappear.

What's happening is you're riding in the red. When you ride in the red too long, you start to link your happiness to the goal. You're depending on the goal to bring you happiness, forgetting you already have access to an unlimited amount of happiness. You can experience happiness anytime you want!

I want teens to understand that pursuing anything worthwhile will have its ups and downs. They'll hit bumps in the road that may not have them feeling good, but they still can feel happiness anytime during the pursuit of goals.

When we're "riding in the red," we need to notice the signs our feelings are giving us. ***Pay attention to your feelings. Since happiness comes before success,*** it's necessary to recognize when you're feeling unhappy, in doubt, discouraged, or other emotional signals that say, *I'm not enough, I'm not going to make it.*

Unhappiness is a sign you're in the red. Take a break and focus on all the things that are good in your life. Once you make the choice to lower your RPMs, you'll start to experience happiness and then you're back on the road to pursuing your goal.

Happiness allows us to be who we were created to be

In my teen coaching, I take the concept of happiness into a deeper place, which really inspires a lot of "aha" moments. Some adults think teens aren't ready to handle concepts of happiness, purpose and meaning, but I find kids are searching and they're ready to go deep to understand themselves and their lives!

I believe every human was created with a purpose and for a purpose. We know from nature how every creature, no matter how big or small, has a purpose, so it shouldn't be much of a stretch for teens to believe they have one too, that there's meaning to who they are and what they do. In the same way no two snowflakes are exactly alike, each of us is unique. We each can do things in our world only we are meant to do.

Happiness allows us to be who we were created to be. Happiness allows us to positively impact those around us in our special way. Happiness is about being caring and kind to others, and about receiving as well as creating positive thoughts.

Another way to explain happiness to teens is to point out its opposite. When we're unhappy, we contract and focus only on ourselves, like a turtle pulling into its shell. When we're unhappy, we forget we're special and unique, or that we could have any kind of impact on others. We get stuck in negativity, which keeps us feeling emotions like self-doubt, anxiety, anger, sadness and even hate. We stop having fun, doing exciting things, or interacting with our friends and family in ways that bring us laughter.

I ask teens, *which would you choose—happiness or unhappiness? Guess what—you DO get to choose to be happy, whenever you want!* You can be happy when eating vegetables and happy when there's no dessert. You can be happy while washing dishes and sitting quietly in class. You can choose to be happy when someone tells you *yes* OR *no.*

Happiness is always available, and it's an inside job. It doesn't necessarily mean we're having the time of our lives; it's simply having positive thoughts. Here's where the P-lens can lend a hand for teens: What P-lens can they choose so they can have a positive perception of something like, well, going to an orthodontist appointment, or taking a tough math test?

Teens need to consciously build skills to get them through life's ups and downs. Figuring out how to stay happy and positive through disappointment, grief, broken bones, and other unimaginable situations is a true superpower.

You reap what you sow

We talked earlier about the adolescent's capacity to see the consequences of their actions, and how their choices impact themselves and others. Teens are ready to learn that things aren't always simple and linear.

Some people see happiness in a transactional way, that it's a give-and-take kind of "scorecard." Most of us have heard the phrase, "you reap what you sow" and interpret it as some type of threatening payback, as if the universe tracks all the times we wronged others so it can create opportunities for us to be wronged in the future.

I believe if this were the case, there would be no good in the world! I think the phrase has a much simpler, even literal meaning: planting seeds in a field. Every time we plant a seed, does it grow? No! Every time we're mean to someone, we don't always receive the same in return. It's not a one-to-one ratio. Someone could wrong us and never pay for their mistake.

Generally, when someone plants a seed, they plant more than one. So if someone has a habit of mistreating people, they'll likely experience more stress and worry in their life. In other words, ***the more seeds of discord, malice, and retaliation they sow, the more likely they will reap the same crop.*** Not because of some magical force, but simple math. It's a game of probability. This is what I tell the teens I work with about consequences of behavior and the path to happiness. The discussion goes like this:

Teen Talk

Dr. RJ: If you cheat on a test every chance you get, eventually you'll get caught. If you constantly lie, others will eventually recognize you as a liar and not trust you anymore.

The concept of reaping and sowing is less about individual actions and more about cultivating habits of positive thinking, sowing seeds of smiles, laughter, kindness, compassion, forgiveness, and love. It's still a probability game, without a one-to-one ratio of return. But sowing and nurturing positive seeds make you feel good, which makes others feel good, which is part of your purpose in living a fabulous life. You can't always know how you've impacted someone in a positive way—but you are.

I often receive positive comments from my teen clients and/or their parents about the results of our work together, and it makes me so happy! What a gift to discover that I've had a positive impact on one of them! I sow the seeds of positive thoughts and emotions, and wherever they grow and whenever I harvest them is a constant surprise and delight.

This is what I call a Happiness State of Mind.

How to cultivate a Happiness State of Mind

Here is how I explain the Happiness State of Mind to my teenagers:

If you have a habit of arguing, then over time you'll reap more arguments and fights. If you make a habit of retaliating when someone wrongs you, you'll reap contention in your life. On the other hand, if you make a habit of giving and being kind, then you'll reap the benefits of kindness.

If you compliment people, chances are you'll receive compliments in return. If you yell and scream at people, eventually you'll get yelled and screamed at in return. Maybe not in a one-to-one ratio, but in a way that colors your life and perspective in one direction or the other.

It's common sense! So how can we use reaping and sowing to our benefit? By interrupting the cycle of negative habits and cultivating a cycle of positive habits.

My lessons for teens—and for all of us: Try to fight the natural tendency to repay anger with anger, jealousy with jealousy, or hurt with hurt. If someone wrongs you, it's your ego's natural impulse to retaliate. Fight the urge to do so. Interrupt the pattern that only perpetuates bad feelings and results, and don't plant seeds of contention. Instead, take the opportunity to plant seeds of forgiveness, and you'll harvest plenty of joy and happiness.

In Chapter 10 we talked about "intrinsic motivation." We could call positive reaping "intrinsic happiness," driven by internal rewards. Behavior that arises not from what we'll GET in return, but because it's naturally satisfying to us.

Powerful concept for teens, isn't it?

In the same way intrinsic motivation is an inside job, embedded in our core to guide everything we do without depending on external rewards, so is intrinsic happiness an inside job. Our teens have the capacity to develop this inner sense of happiness that isn't tied to external rewards, perceptions, judgments, or instant gratification. It's tied to the truth they know about themselves, the choices they make from the clear knowledge of what's right for them, and comes from their self-confidence and self-love.

Deep down smiles on the inside AND the outside!

Final thoughts on pursuing happiness

Talking about achieving happiness naturally brings up its own judgments and pressures, which leads me to share what Ruth Whippman says in her book, *America the Anxious: How Our Pursuit of Happiness Is Creating a Nation of Nervous Wrecks*[32]: "My instinct is that...happiness should be serendipitous, the by-product of a life well lived, and chasing it in a vacuum just doesn't really work." This is an excellent point, especially for teens developing the experience, perspective, and discernment to think about what happiness looks like.

Some teens come to me in such an anxious and unhappy state, because they're *trying* to do all the "right" things to achieve the accomplishments they think they want: getting into the "best" schools, winning awards and

---

[32] https://www.amazon.com/gp/product/1250071526

scholarships, getting ahead. None of these are bad things to aspire to, but some teens are becoming the nervous wrecks from Whippman's book title, and I'm not sure "happiness" even enters their mind. Many of these anxious teens have a parent or two behind them, pushing and pressuring them.

I'm not questioning whether or not the reasons are valid, but when these teens obsess over *objects* and *events* that are going to "make" them happy, what are they sacrificing in their well-being and health?

In an opinion article for the *New York Times* called "Happiness Is Other People,"[33] Whippman suggests we look at our relationships and how we connect with others. According to her, yes, happiness comes from within, but she finds too many people are turning to isolated practices and lifestyles in order to reach happiness, to the exclusion of community.

I agree we need the balance outside of ourselves by having meaningful relationships. Whippman cites research that this is true across race, gender, income, and social class: "the strongest, most consistent predictor there is of a happy life."

This is why I counsel teens on "the missing piece of success." When they expand their P-lens to include people and relationships they've overlooked, they find help and support to accomplish their goals from unexpected, enriching places. AND, so much more importantly, they'll be reaching out to their community and developing relationships that will help them grow inside and out.

This is also why I spend so much time coaching teens on their relationships with others, building self-confidence, and learning how to have open, honest communication. My hope is they'll learn happiness is always available to them, and they can welcome happiness into their lives both from within and in community with others.

Let's do what we can to support our teenagers in balancing the different aspects that bring happiness to their lives!

---

[33] https://www.nytimes.com/2017/10/27/opinion/sunday/happiness-is-other-people.html

How to help your teen welcome happiness into their life

1. Bolster their understanding that life naturally has ups and downs, ebbs and flows, and they have control over their response. As long as they are working with their thoughts, feelings, and actions in a conscious, productive way, they'll have the ability to face any challenges that arise. They don't have to see anxiety, depression, or self-destructive behavior as options.

2. Happiness is always available to them. Many teens believe happiness is found in things "outside" themselves rather than in thoughts and beliefs they hold. Sharing the concepts in this chapter can help them begin to see happiness through a more expansive P-lens. Find small moments of the day where you can point out that your teen IS happiness, not that they will GET happiness.

3. Talk about receiving and creating positive thoughts. This is a powerful way to get teens to develop habits based on positive thinking. The Thought Triangle and P-lens both reinforce the practice of paying attention to thoughts that make kids feel good, and the actions and results they experience because of those thoughts. "Happiness" becomes less of an endgame and more of a surprising, feel-good icing on the cake!

4. Give your teen opportunities to be caring to others. If an opportunity comes around to do something kind for someone else, suggest it to your teen (gently, don't pressure—they have to own their motivation). Not for a resume-builder or to harvest a reward, but for the feel-good happiness they'll give and receive. Generosity feeds intrinsic happiness, so empower your teen with this important idea: *You reap what you sow, so choose to sow positive seeds and watch them grow.*

If you believe you and/or your adolescent could benefit from life coaching, use this code to schedule a consultation.

Conclusion

Well, quite a journey we've taken together, wouldn't you say?

We've covered a lot of ground on the foundations that will guide our teenagers through adolescence with awareness, confidence, and (I truly hope) more self-love, to become adults we can be proud of and, most importantly, adults THEY can be proud of.

I want to wrap things up with a summary of some of my key teachings when it comes to empowering teens. I hope you've enjoyed learning about them in this book, and that you'll apply them to the relationship with your teen:

*The teen years are critical because this is when foundations for adulthood are built. If issues aren't resolved now, the teen will continue to struggle with them as they get older.

*If your child is NOT actively developing their confidence, then your child is NOT confident. True confidence needs to be developed and practiced.

*A teen's experience of life begins with their thoughts and beliefs.

*My vision for teens is for them to focus on everything that makes them feel good about themselves. They have the ability to wire their brains for a positive outlook.

*When teens are confident, they'll tap into their full potential, fulfilling the purpose for which they were created.

*Positive thoughts help you thrive. They speak joy, love, happiness, forgiveness, and other good things. When these thoughts affect your behavior, your mind grows.

*Any belief that keeps you from unlocking your potential is a limiting belief.

*Your perceptions color your world and interpret the events of your life. You get to choose the ones that build your happiness.

*How we handle disappointment is how we'll handle any obstacles in our lives.

*The reason teenagers, even high-performing ones, suffer from anxiety is FEAR.

*What we think about is what we feel, which is what we focus on. Don't we want those thoughts to make us feel good about ourselves?

*Work on trusting, understanding, and respecting your teen and they'll return in kind.

*The relationships teens develop will determine their overall level of happiness each day.

*Teach your teen to use their words wisely, because words have the power to build up or destroy.

*Your words as a parent affect your teen's developing self-esteem more than anything else!

*The power of goals is to shift focus away from holding a teen back toward getting what they really want.

*Treat everyone as if they were the missing piece to your success.

*Purpose, meaning, and happiness are what we strive for in life, and must be behind our definitions of success.

*Leadership is living our fullest potential.

*Happiness is a state of mind where we either receive or create positive thoughts.

*Happiness allows us to be who we were created to be.

THANK YOU for leaning in to support the teens in your life. I hope this book has been supportive, informative, and empowering. I would love to stay connected and I encourage you to check out the following resources for you and your teens:

Website: https://drrjjackson.com/

Weekly podcast: A Teen's Perspective

Join Dr. RJ's Facebook group: https://www.facebook.com/dr.rjjackson

Learn about Life Scholars Academy coaching program for parents: https://lifescholarsacademy.com/

Remember, happiness and confidence are an inside job!

Acknowledgments

First and foremost, all praise and glory to my Father in Heaven and Yeshua (Jesus), His son.

Next, I want to thank the most important woman in this world to me, my wife, Frances. You are truly amazing! Thank you for reading this book over a hundred times. Thank you for all the conversations, all the discussion of ideas, and thank you for giving me the thousands of hours to write while you took care of our boys. You are truly a superwoman.

Jeremiah and Isaiah, my sons, I want to thank you for inspiring me each and every day. When I look at you two, I'm reminded that God has a bigger plan for my life.

Thank you, Mama, for your unwavering encouragement. Anytime I had doubts, you constantly reminded me, "all in God's time."

About the Author

Dr. RJ Jackson works with thousands of teenagers through orthodontics, mentoring, community leadership, and as a nationally known, certified Teen Life Coach.

What drives this "Teen Whisperer" is a deep desire for all teenagers to have the opportunity to feel happy and successful. It's a passion that started way back in grade school, when young RJ was the person in whom others felt comfortable confiding their problems.

In middle school, RJ created the first-ever "Student Talks" program, where for 15 minutes a day, students were given the opportunity to speak to teachers, coaches, and guidance counselors about life. With the success of that program, he committed to a lifelong mission of spreading happiness.

Dr. RJ went on to establish an orthodontics practice where he could help young people smile on the outside. It wasn't long before many parents of his patients were asking Dr. RJ to coach their teens through challenges. The intuitive talent he discovered back in sixth grade still had teens sharing things with him they couldn't tell anyone else (including and sometimes especially their parents). Together, they worked through thorny problems, explored their questions, and celebrated great improvements.

These many successes had him hooked. Dr. RJ became a certified Life Coach—one of the few in America specializing in teenagers. Today, he hears the many challenges teenagers face at home, in school, in their activities and relationships, and preparing for their future after high school. He works with teens and parents individually, and offers group coaching calls where he regularly has over a hundred teens on the line from all over the country. With a light touch, humor, and infectious enthusiasm, he tackles the tough questions facing today's teens and teaches straight-talking strategies they can use right away.

Creator and host of the weekly podcast, "A Teen's Perspective," Dr. RJ provides a unique safe space for teens and parents to connect, share, and get professional coaching. He recently launched a program tailored for parents, "Coach Your Own Teen."

Dr. RJ is a sought-after speaker and gives customized seminars and workshops for schools, businesses, and not-for-profit-organizations. In his spare time, Dr. RJ mentors teens at his church, using the core elements of his coaching principles designed to help teens reach the greatness they were created to achieve.

Dr. RJ lives with his family in Austin, Texas, where you can find him creating smiles on the inside and on the outside. His book, *How to Train Your Superhero*, was a #1 international bestseller.

Website: https://drrjjackson.com/
Email: https://drrjjackson.com/
Weekly podcast: A Teen's Perspective
Facebook: https://www.facebook.com/dr.rjjackson
LinkedIn: https://www.linkedin.com/in/dr-rj-jackson-7aa0121a8/

If you believe you and/or your adolescent could benefit from life coaching, use this code to schedule a consultation.

Reviews

"Do you want your teenager to feel happy and successful—inside and out? Look no further than this inspirational book by Dr. RJ. In *Parenting Happy Teens: It's an Inside Job*, Dr. RJ describes his life-long passion of assisting teens and their parents in truly recognizing that "happiness is always available." A motivational resource, Dr. RJ shares with his readers how thoughts, emotions, confidence, communication, and relationships all have a significant impact on helping teenagers (and their parents!) learn to enhance their happiness mindset. Helping teens and their parents focus on living and creating a life with purpose and meaningful goals, this book is must-read for adults, teens, and everyone in between!"
—Wendy K. Benson, MBA, OTR/L and Elizabeth A. Myers, RN
Co-Authors, *The Confident Patient*
2x2 Health: Private Health Concierge
http://www.2x2health.com/

"As a retired teacher, I believe this book should be recommended reading for all parents and teens. It is an easy to read book that is chock full of practical wisdom for everyone. Parents and teenagers will learn effective communication techniques, better relationship skills, and gain a clear sense of who they are and how to relate to each other. The skills taught in *Parenting Happy Teens* help to develop self-confident, successful, happy adults."
—Elda Robinson
Author of *A Simple Cup of -Ty*
Facebook: Bowtie Shoes
Email: Bowtieshoes21@gmail.com

"Working in higher education for 21 years, I have seen a shift in what teens think when it comes to achieving success and happiness. These thoughts have created increased amounts of stress, anxiety, and fatigue as they chase notions of achievement and success that have been externally defined. This is why *Parenting Happy Teens: It's an Inside Job* is so critical to read NOW. Dr. RJ targets where the heart is when it comes to building confidence and accurate thinking within teens. His focus on educating families about how to care for teens so that they can understand their own potential, thinking, and behaviors is truly powerful. Dr. RJ helps families apply their understanding through visuals, tips, and resources designed directly for teens and for those raising them. If you have a tween or teen at home, the time is now to read *Parenting Happy Teens: It's an Inside Job*."

—Sonja Montiel, M.A.
Founder of College Confidence
Co-Founder of The DH Effect
https://www.collegeconfidence.net

Made in the USA
Columbia, SC
29 February 2024

32176868R00078